Sit your ASS down and color

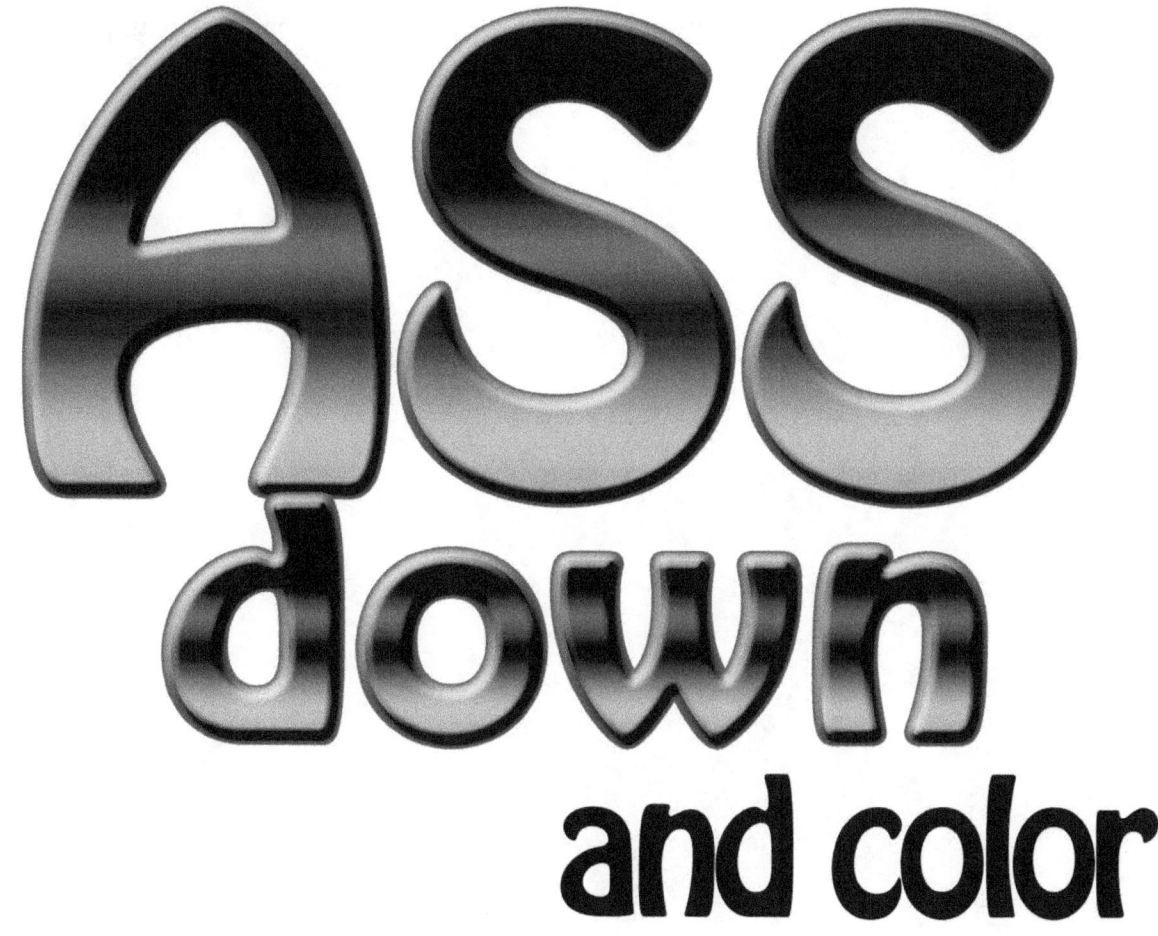

SWEAR WORD ADULT COLORING BOOK

31 ILLUSTRATIONS USING THE WORD ASS

Life is full of things that stress us out. Between work, children, bills, and chores at home, our minds are inundated with stuff vying for our attention. Coloring is a great way to relax and allow stress to melt away.

Have a problem you are trying to figure out? Just open up this book, take your colored pencils, and begin filling in the blank spaces. Don't focus on anything, but coloring what is within this book. By doing this, you will clear you mind, and just might come up with the solution you've been searching for.

With 31 designs, all featuring the word ass, to color, this book has something for every skill level. So just take a moment, relax, and color.

You can tear this page out and use it to put between the images so as to avoid bleed through.

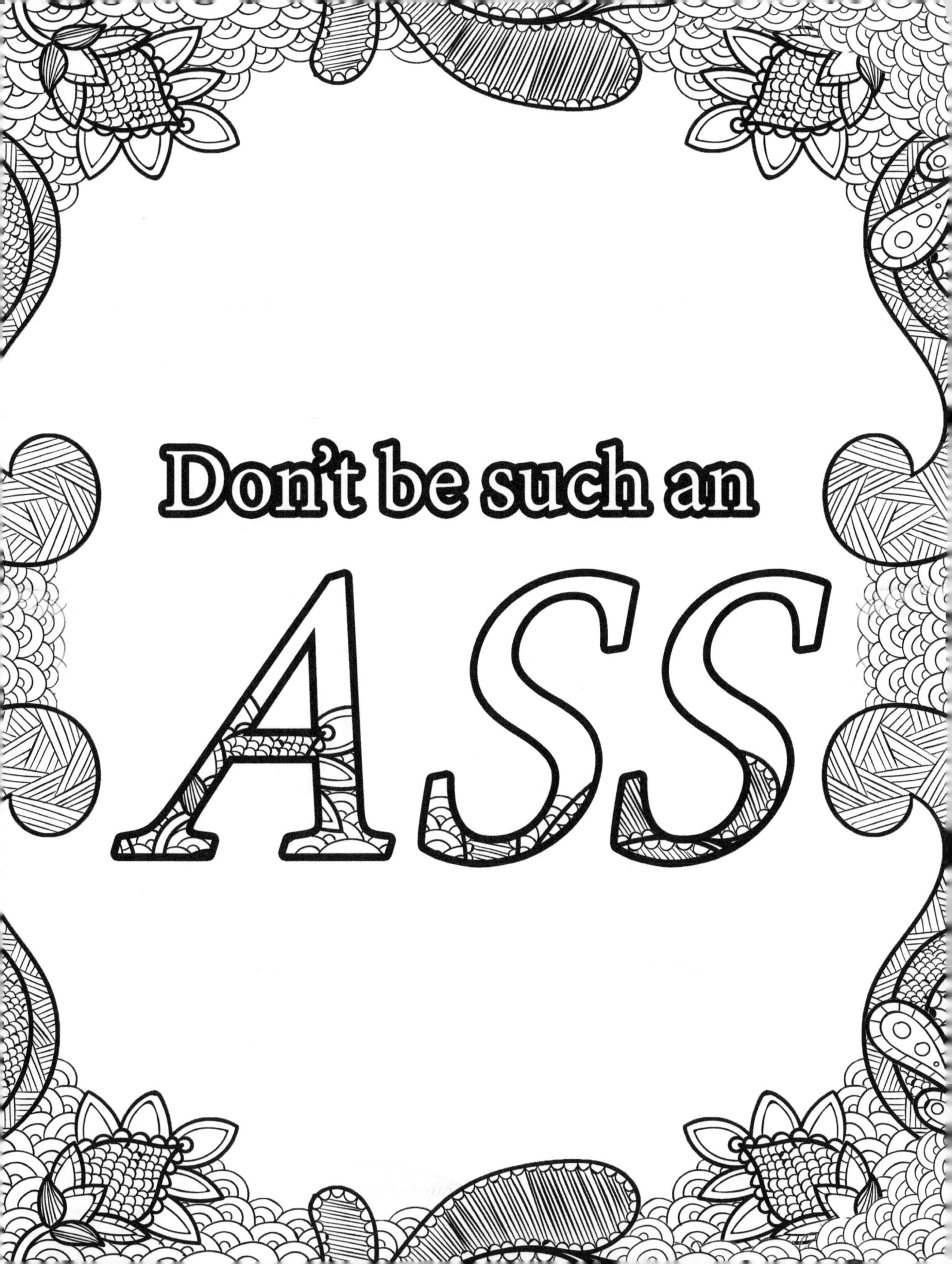

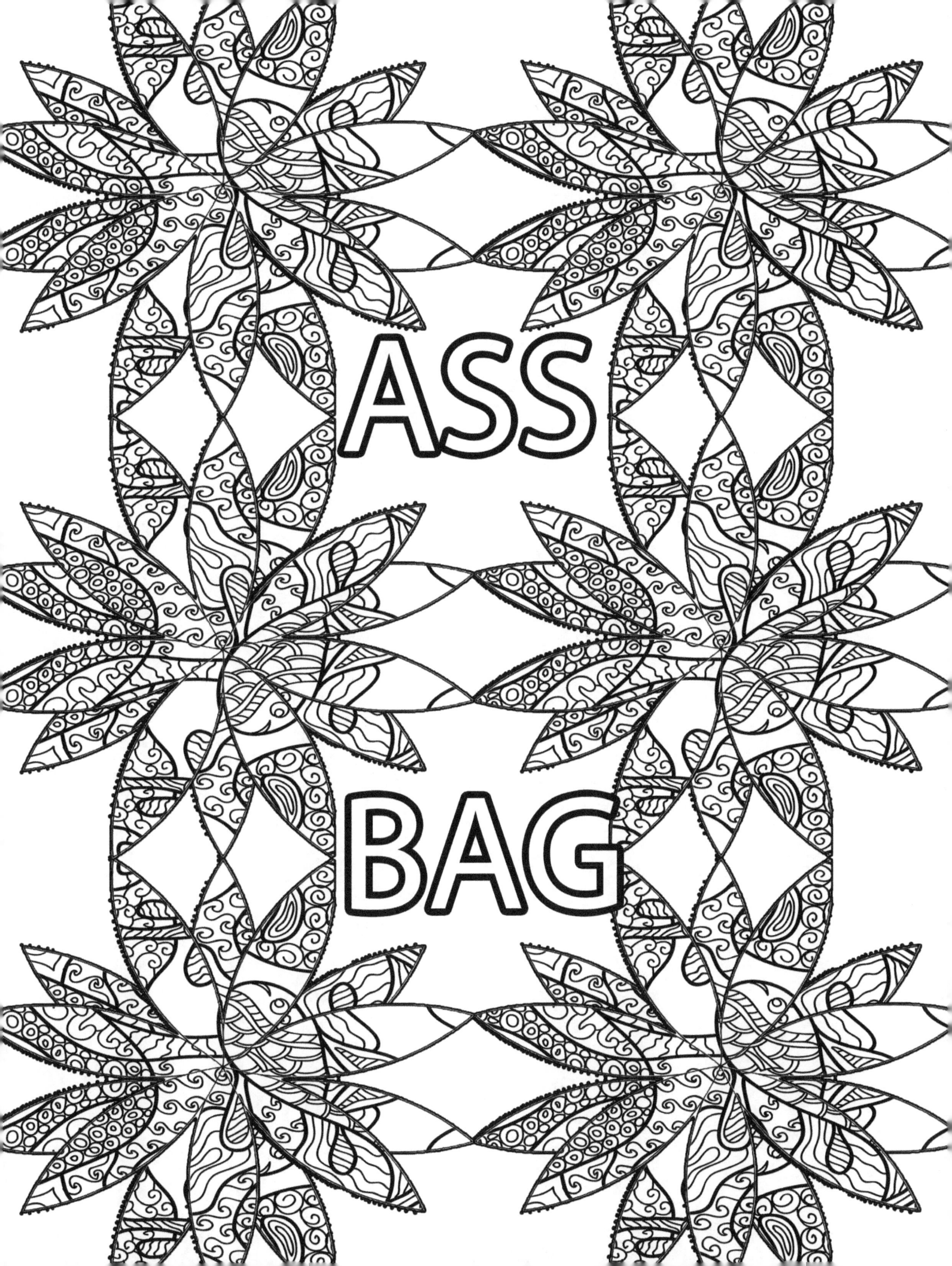

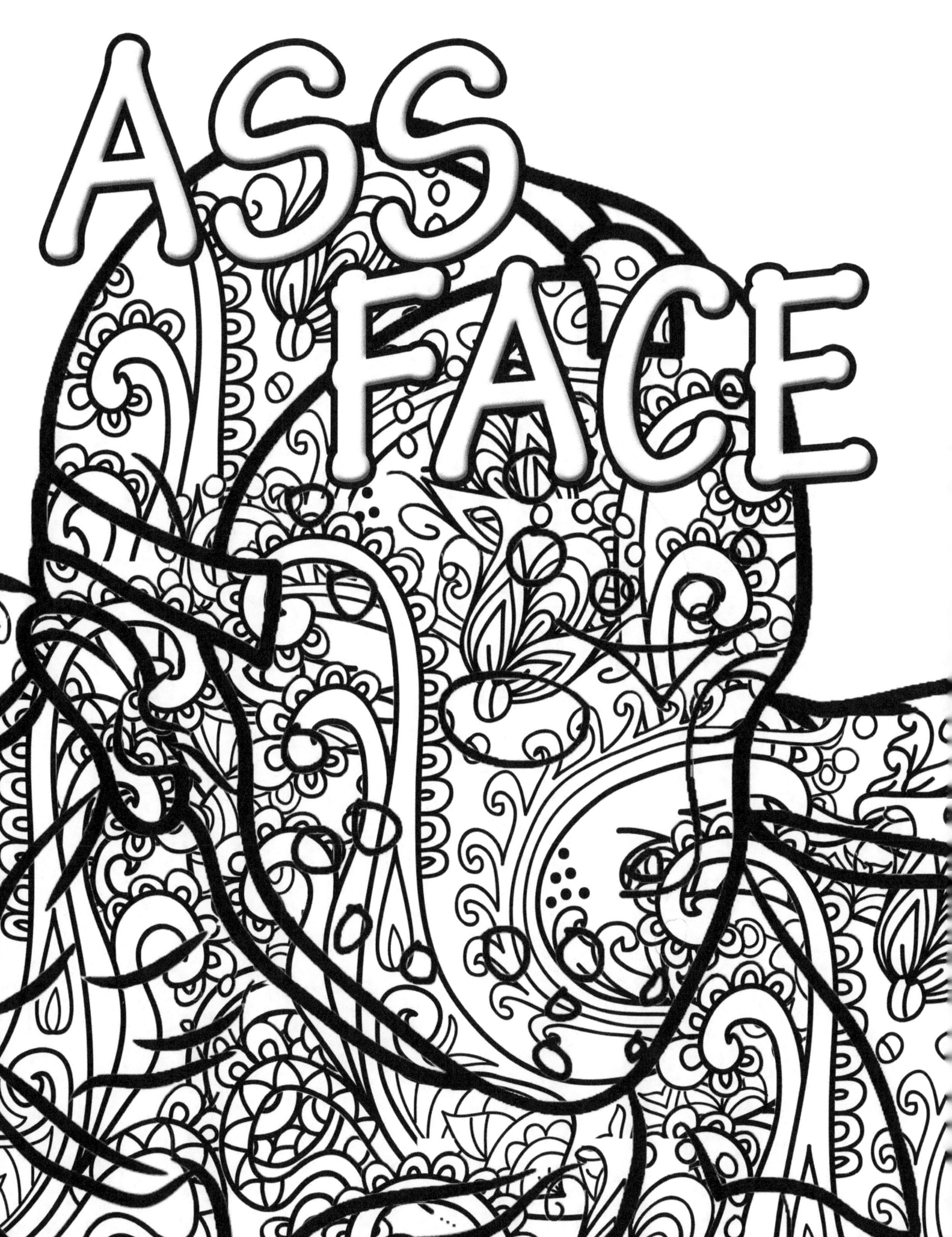

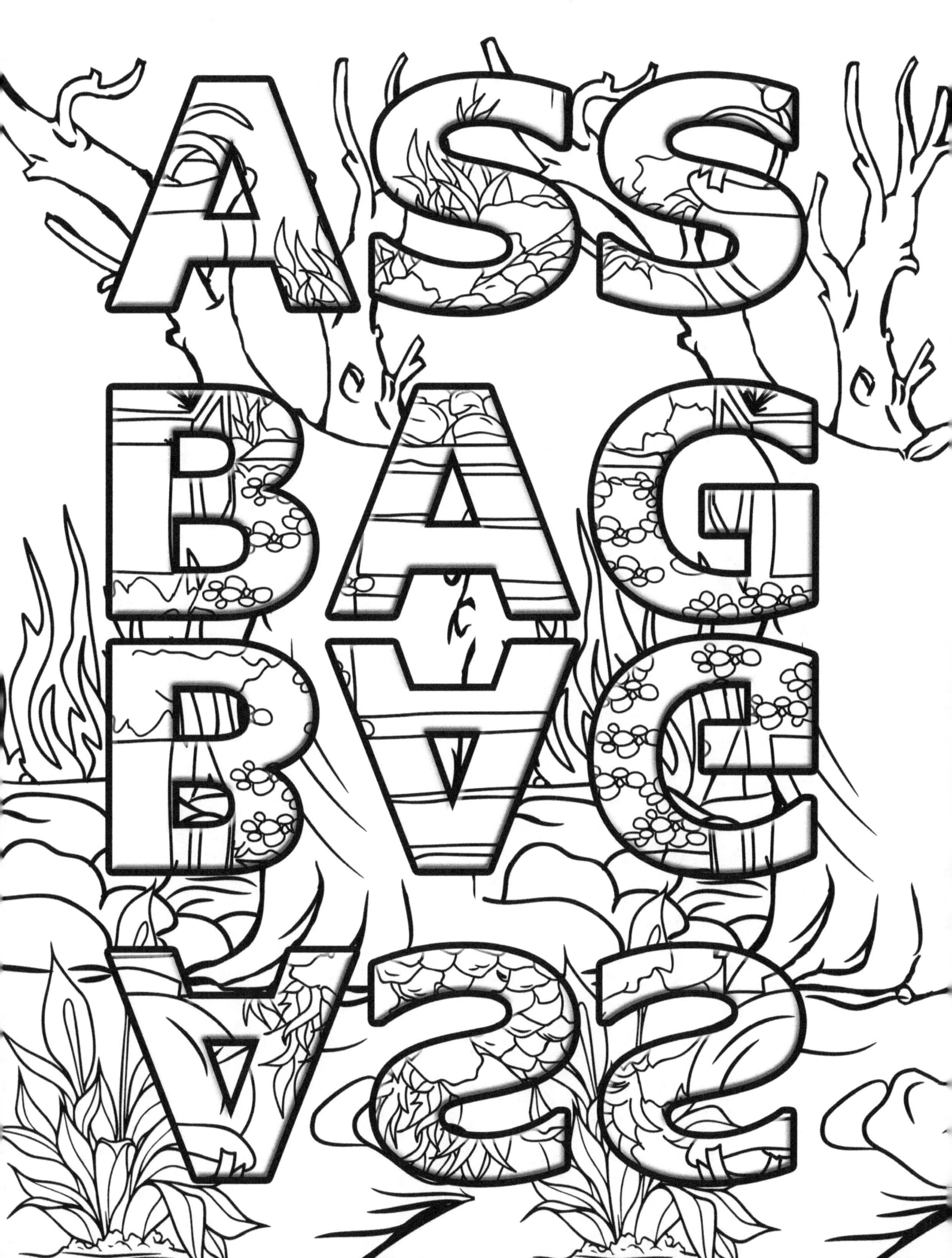

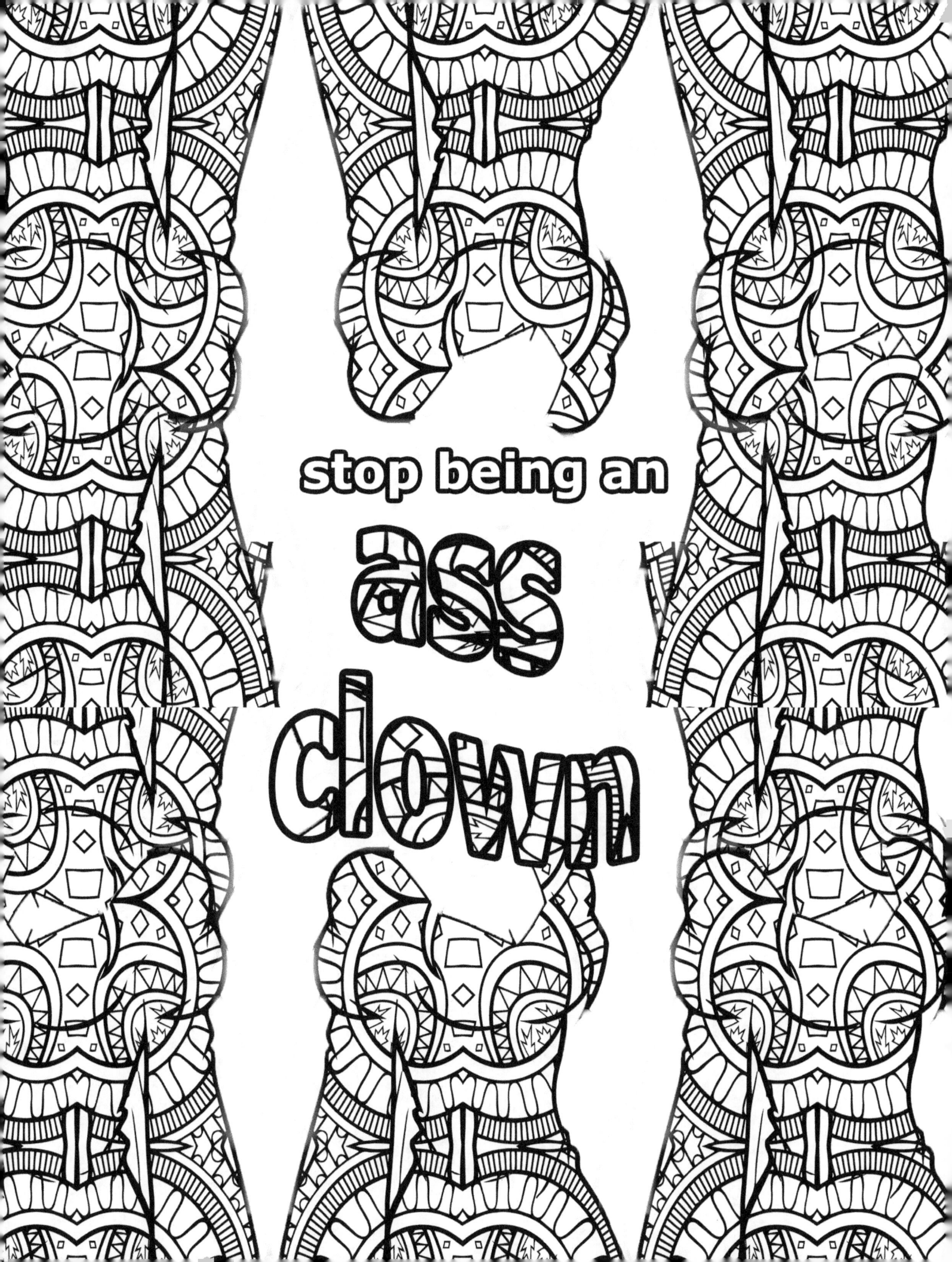

stop being an ass clown

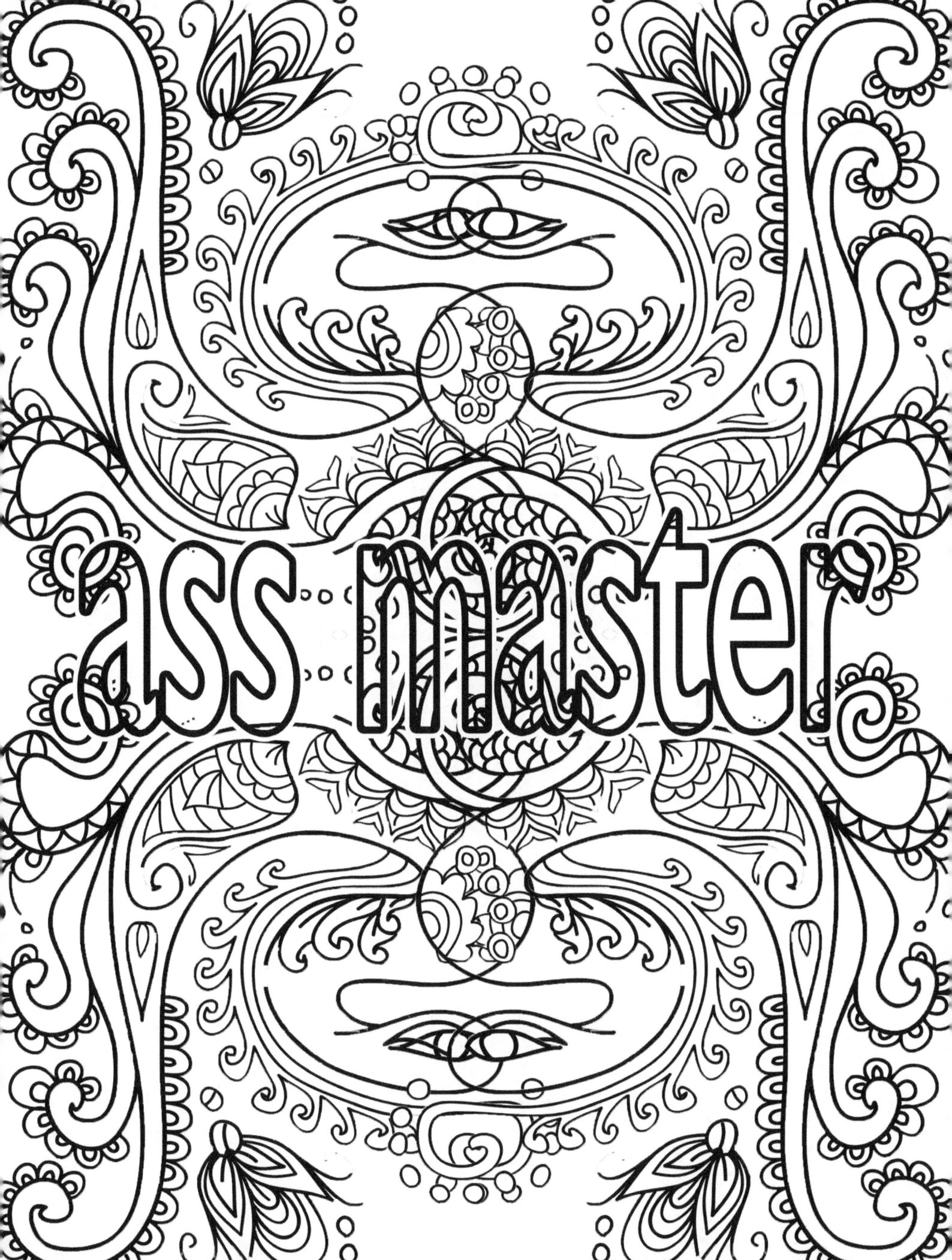

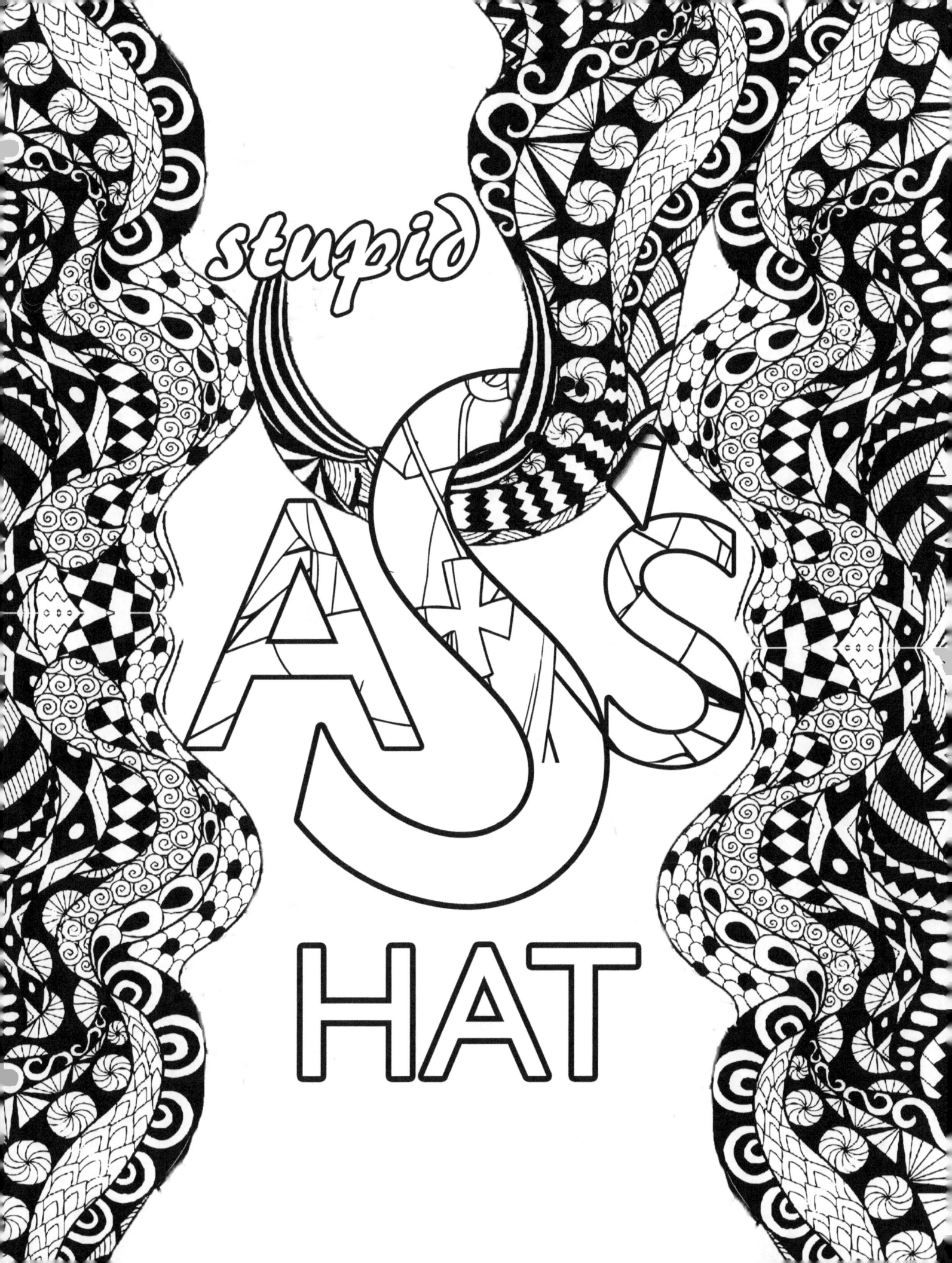

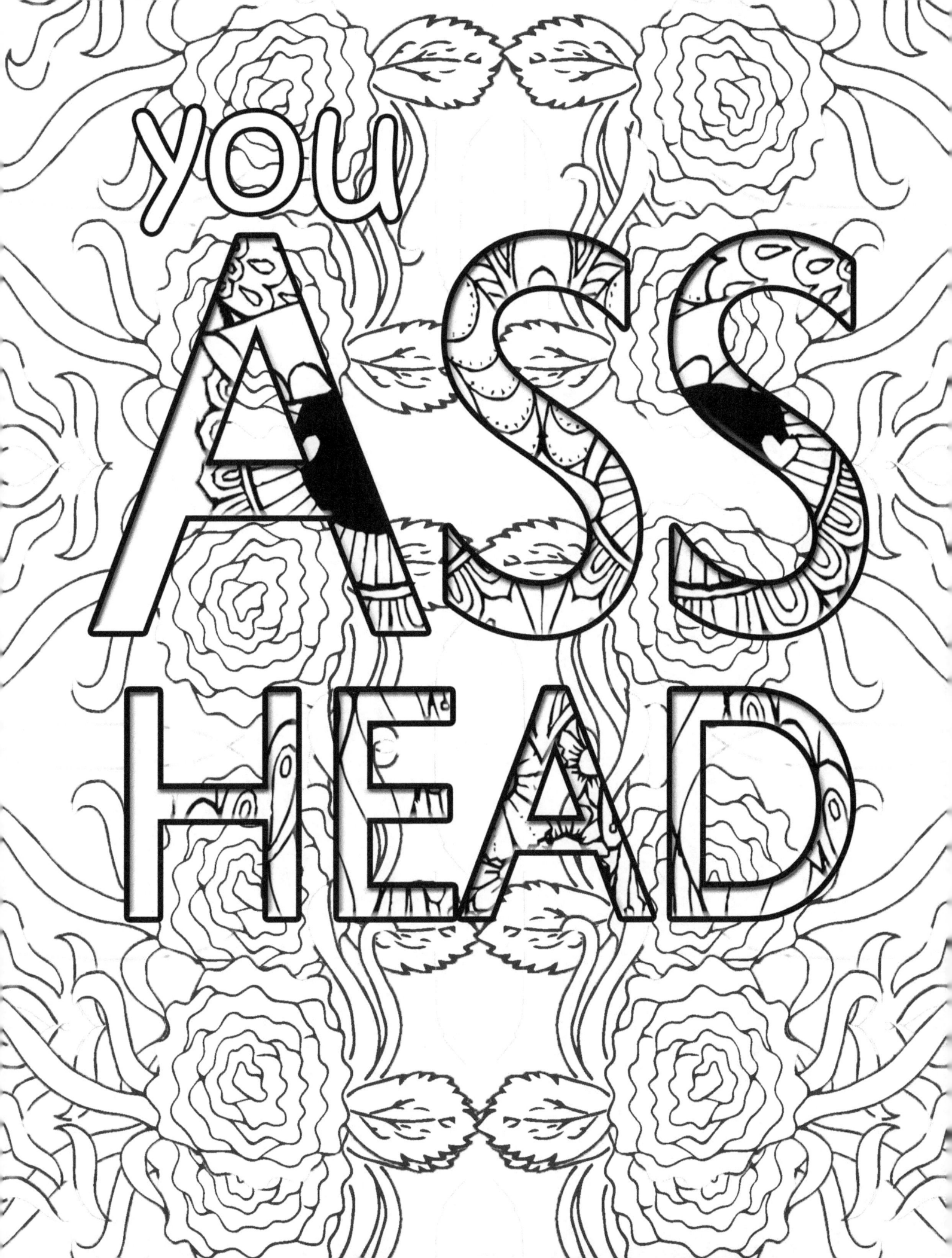

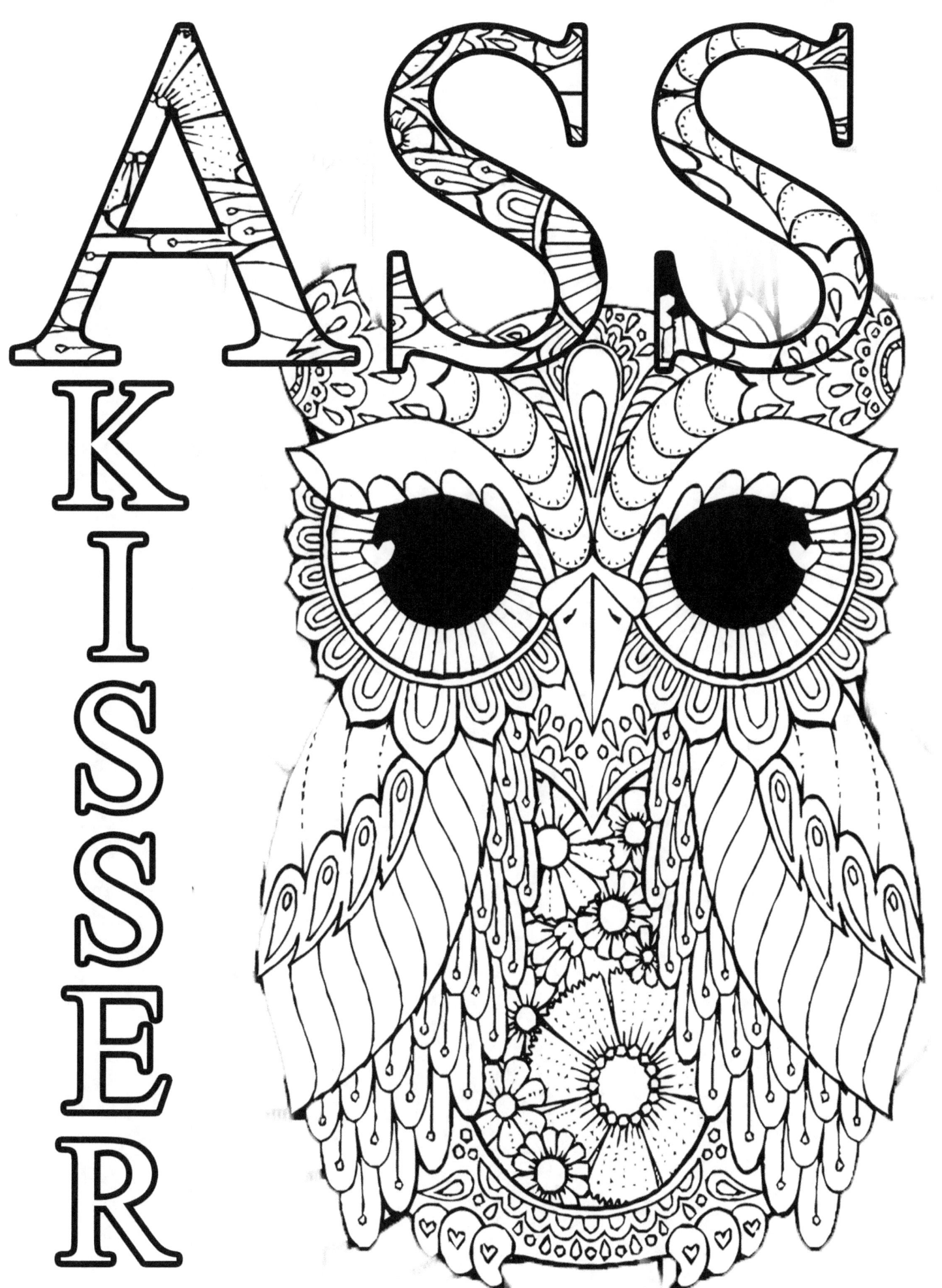

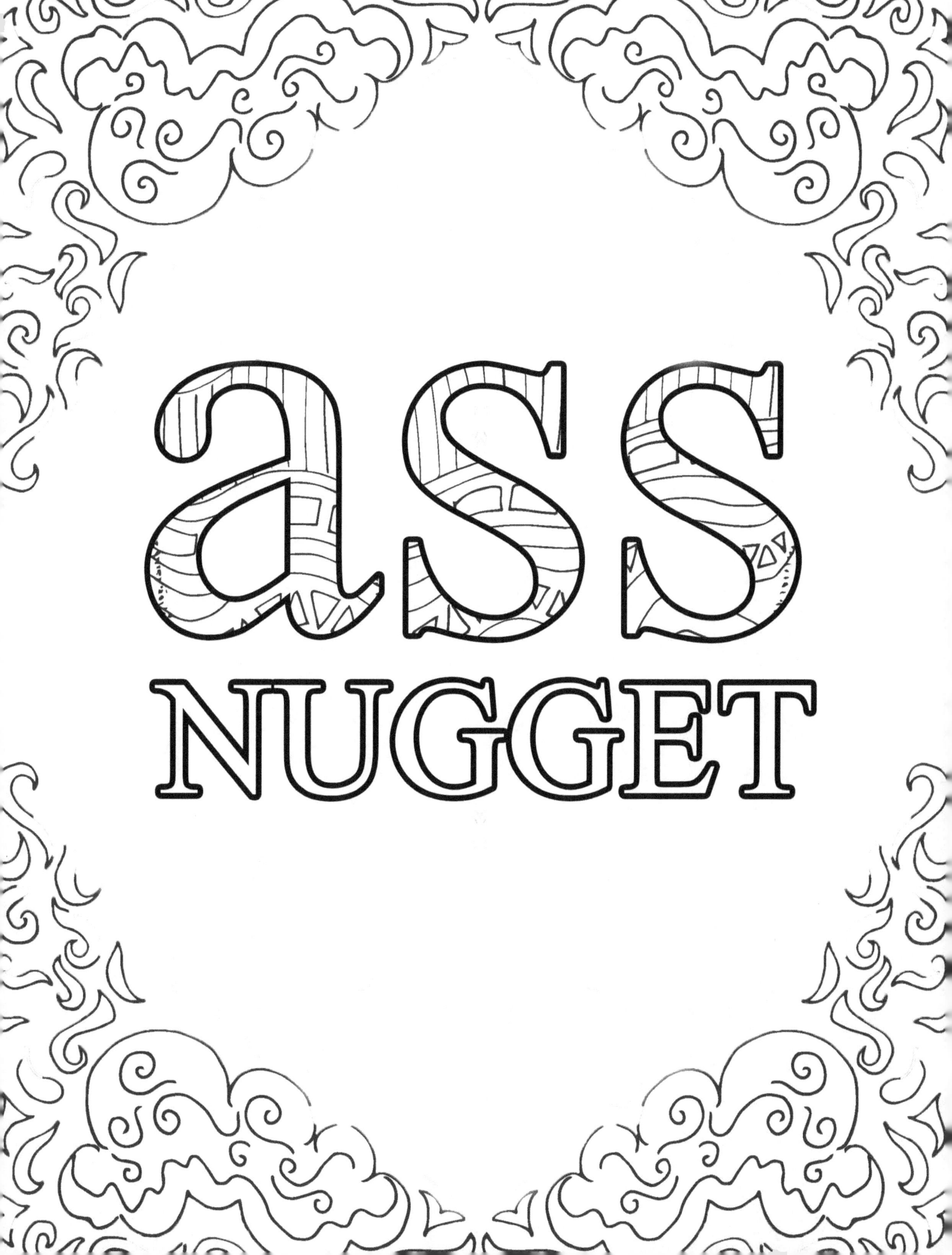

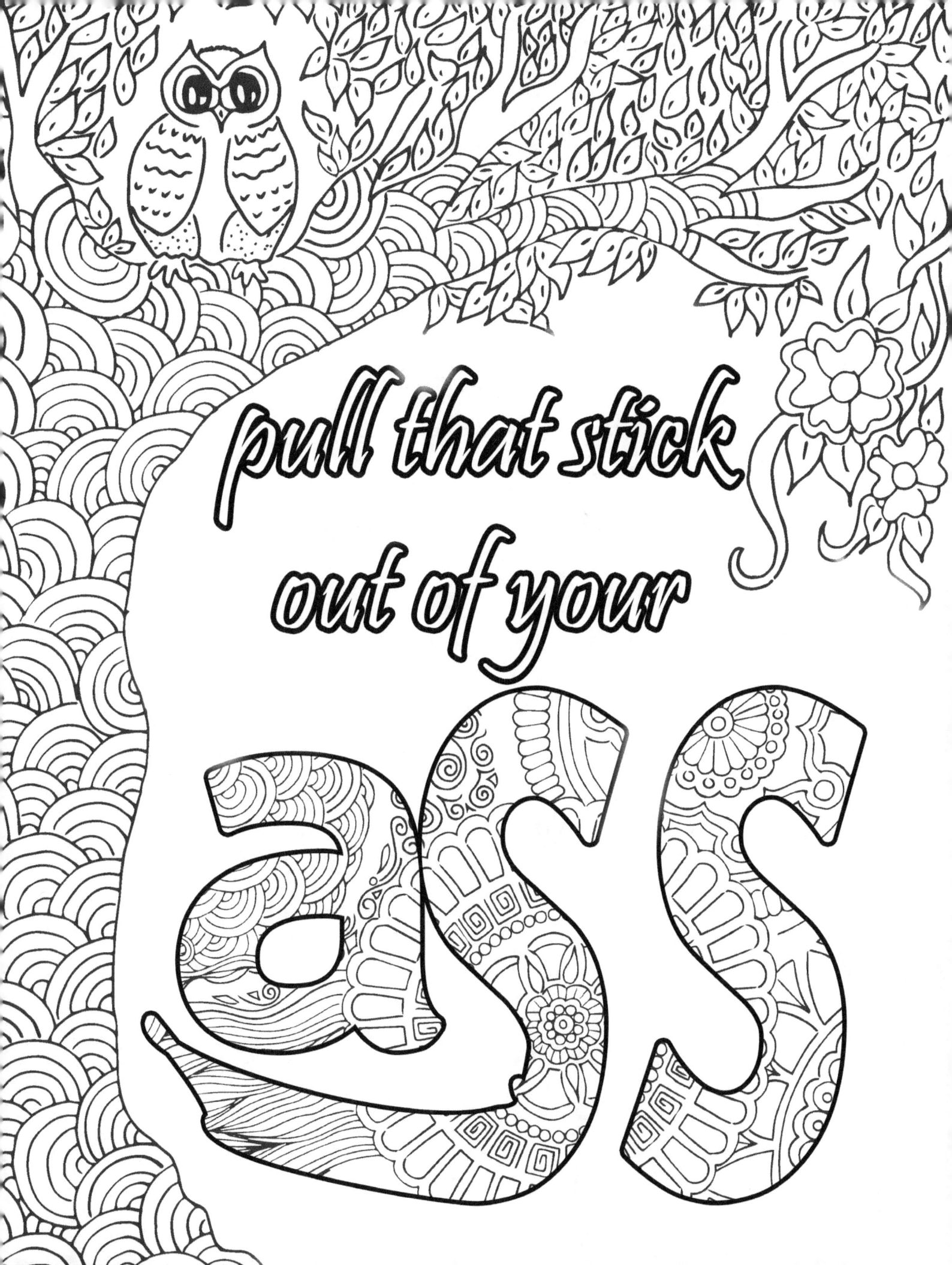

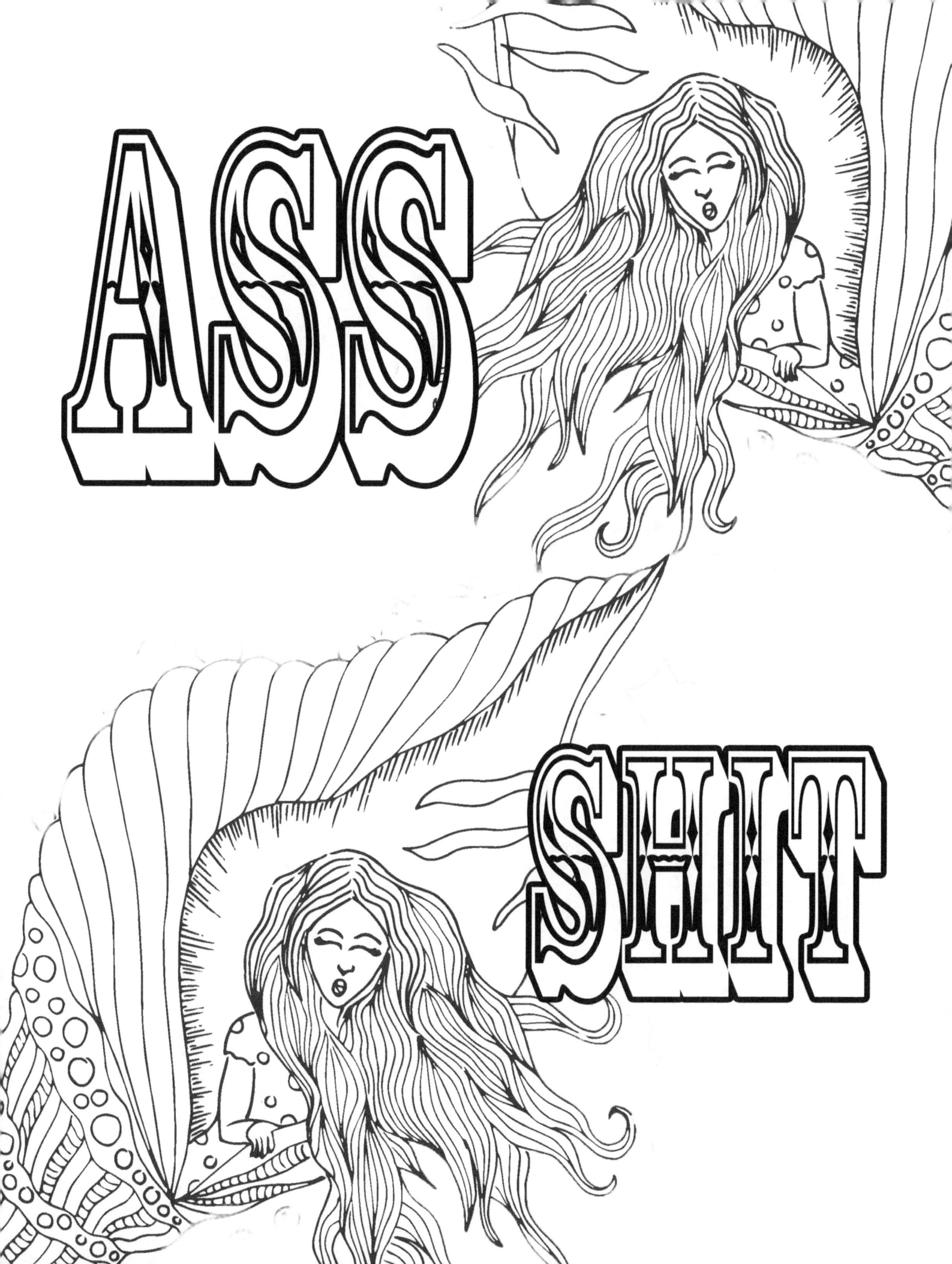

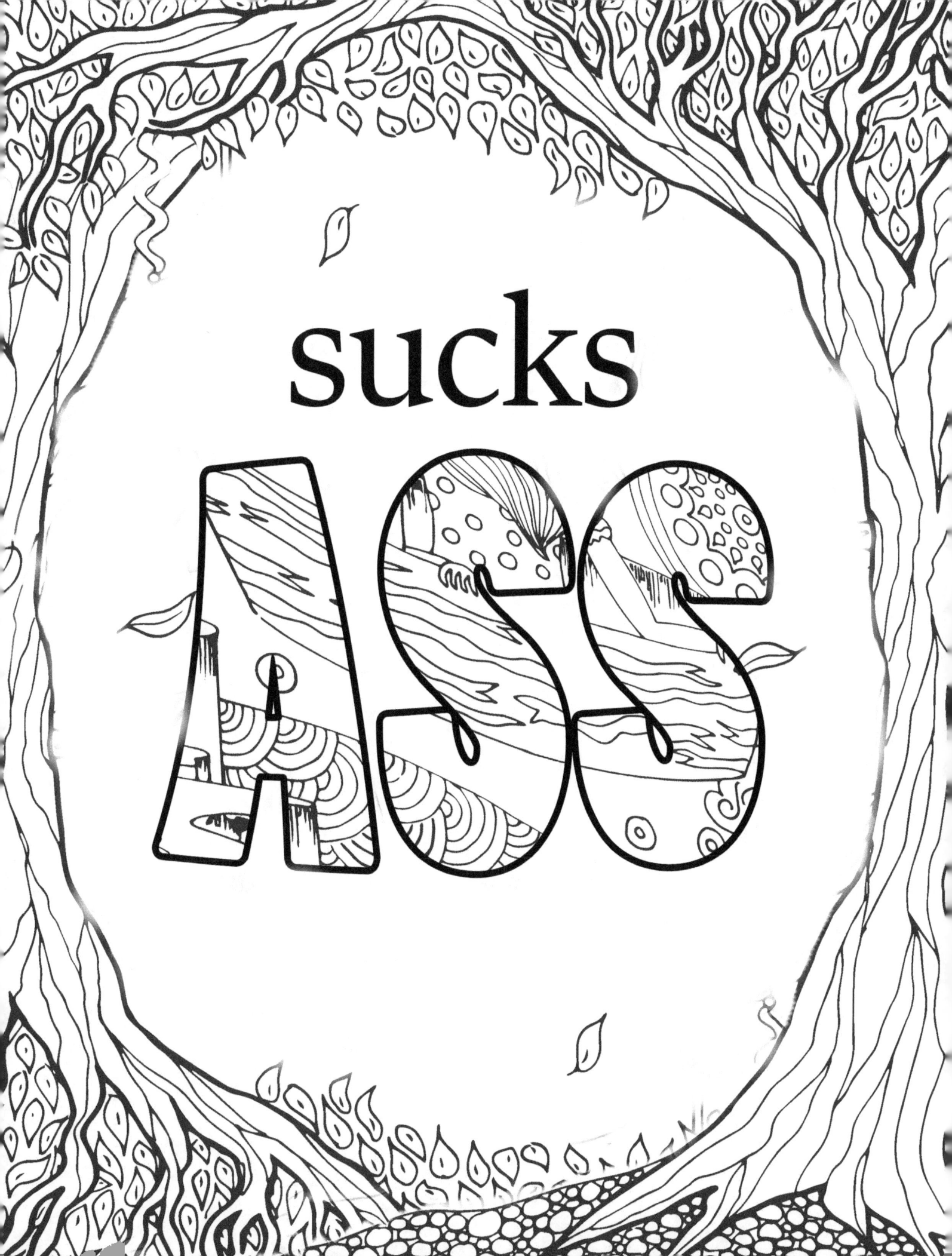

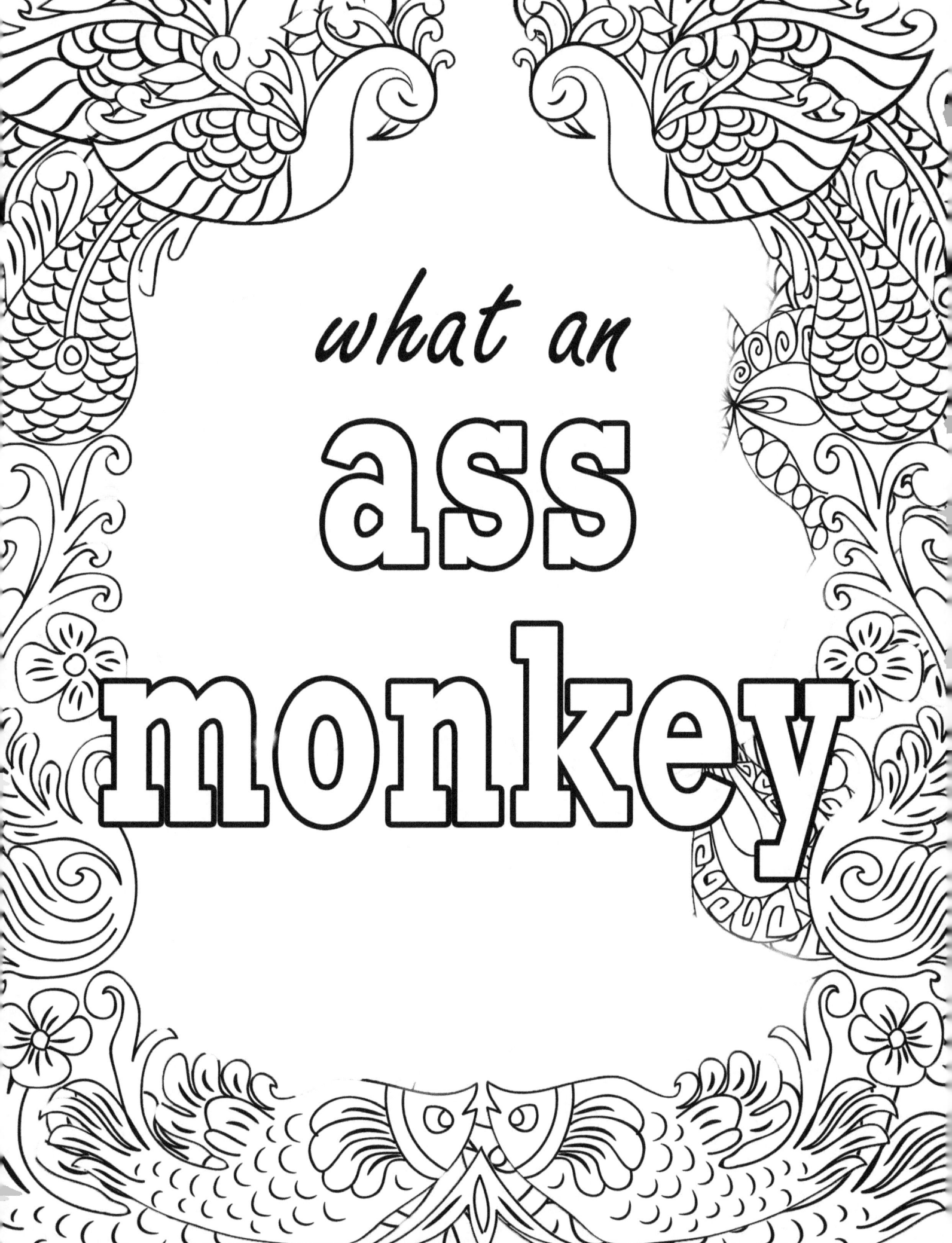

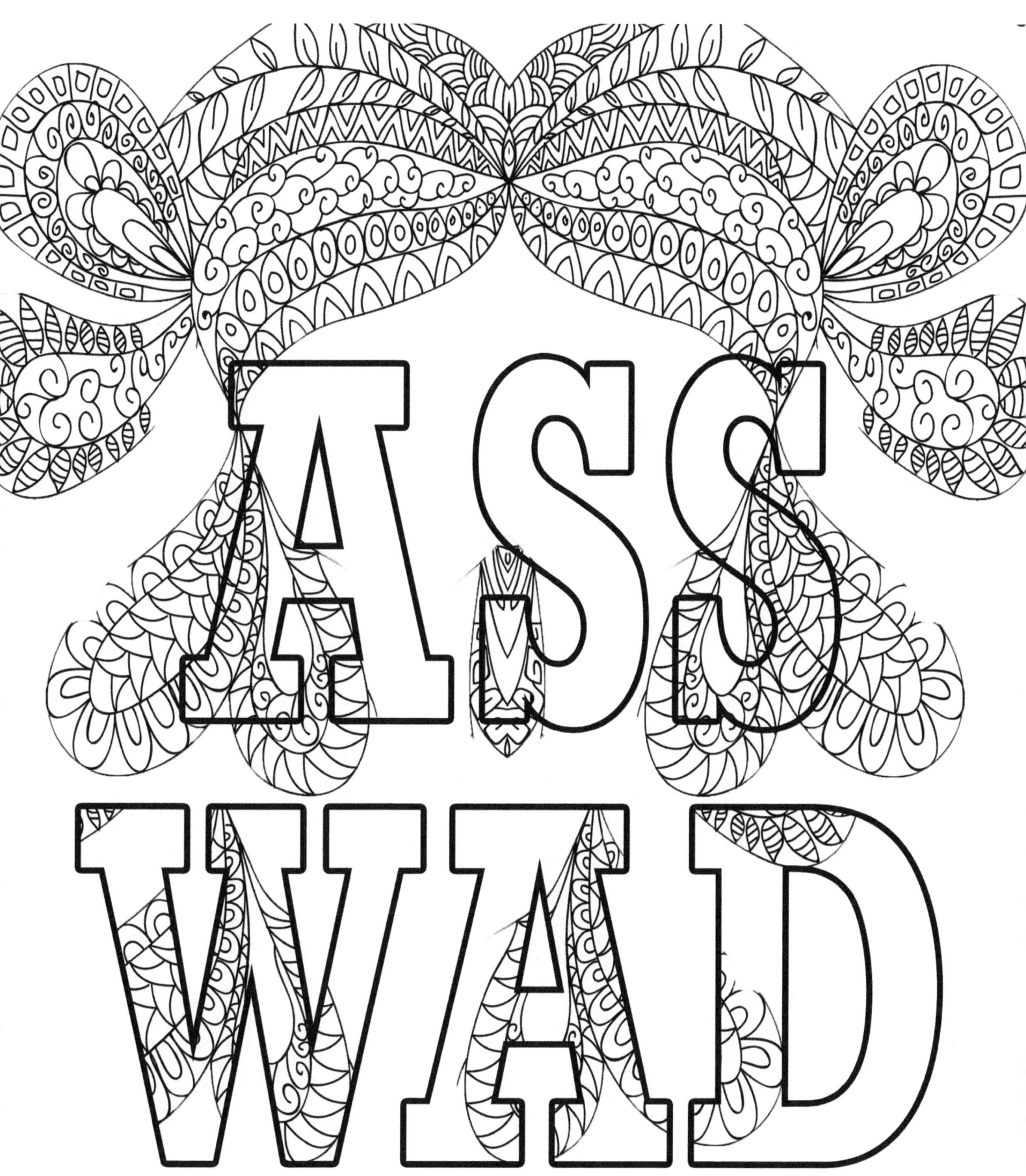

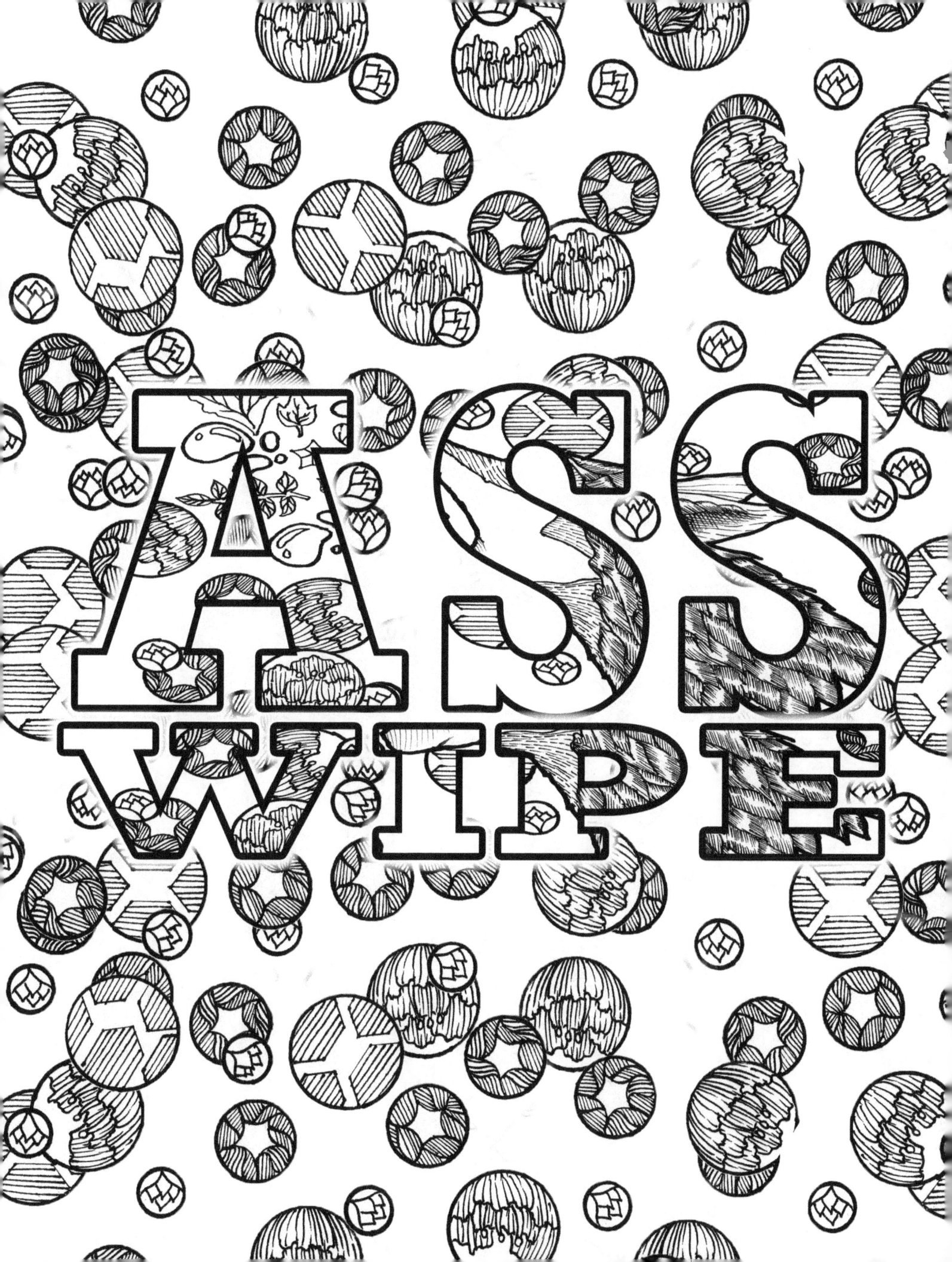

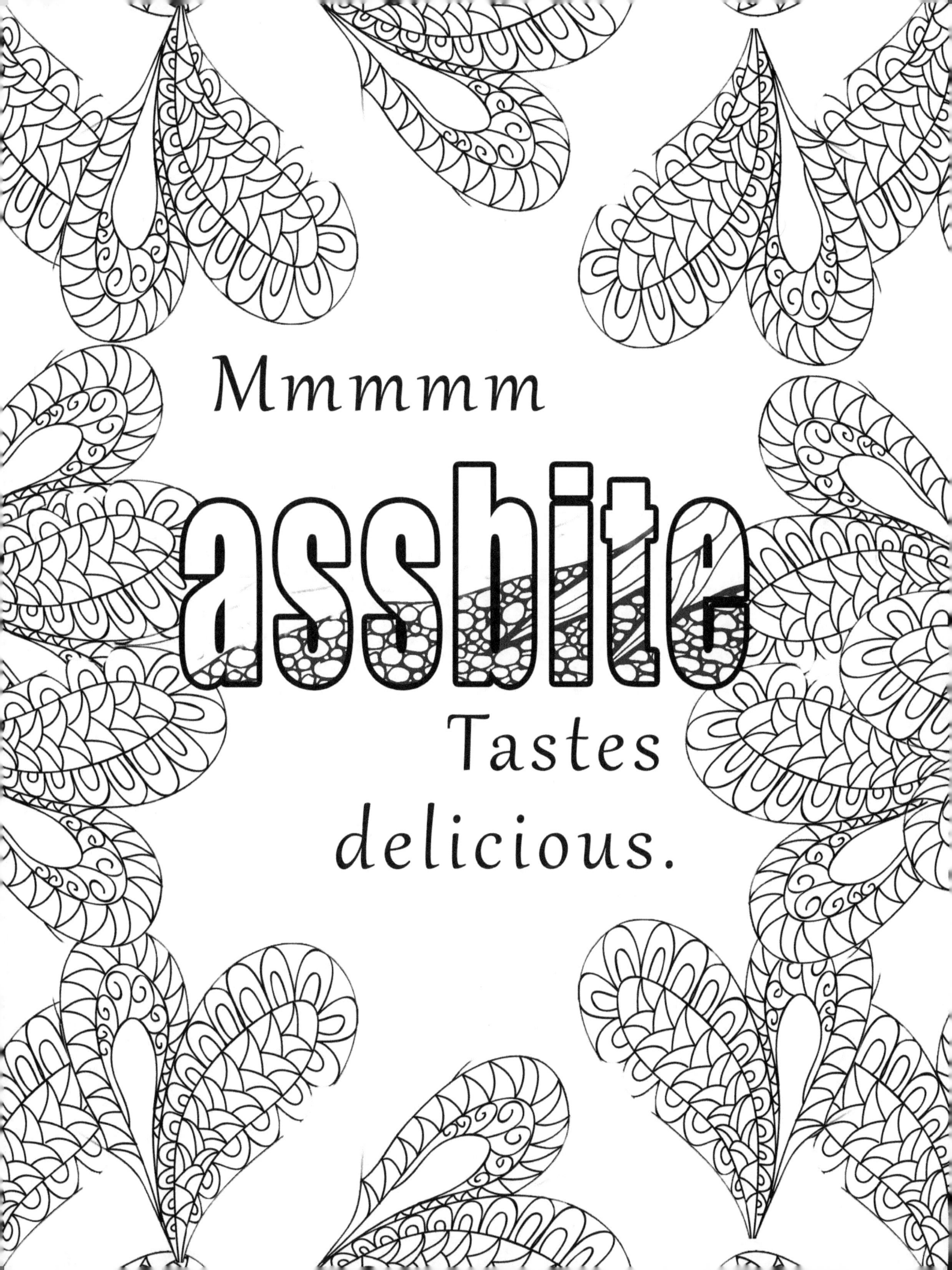

Mmmmm

asshite

Tastes

delicious.

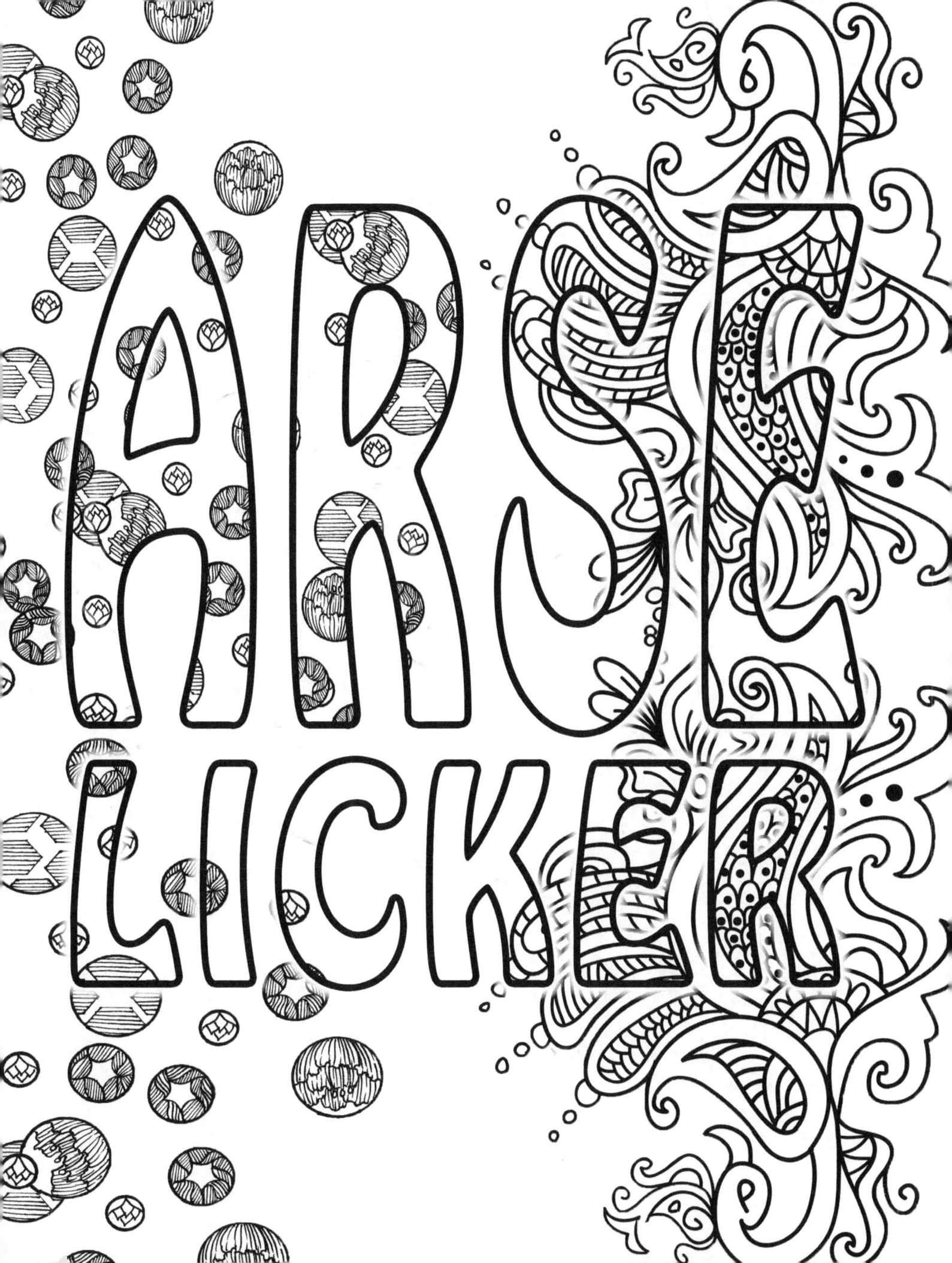

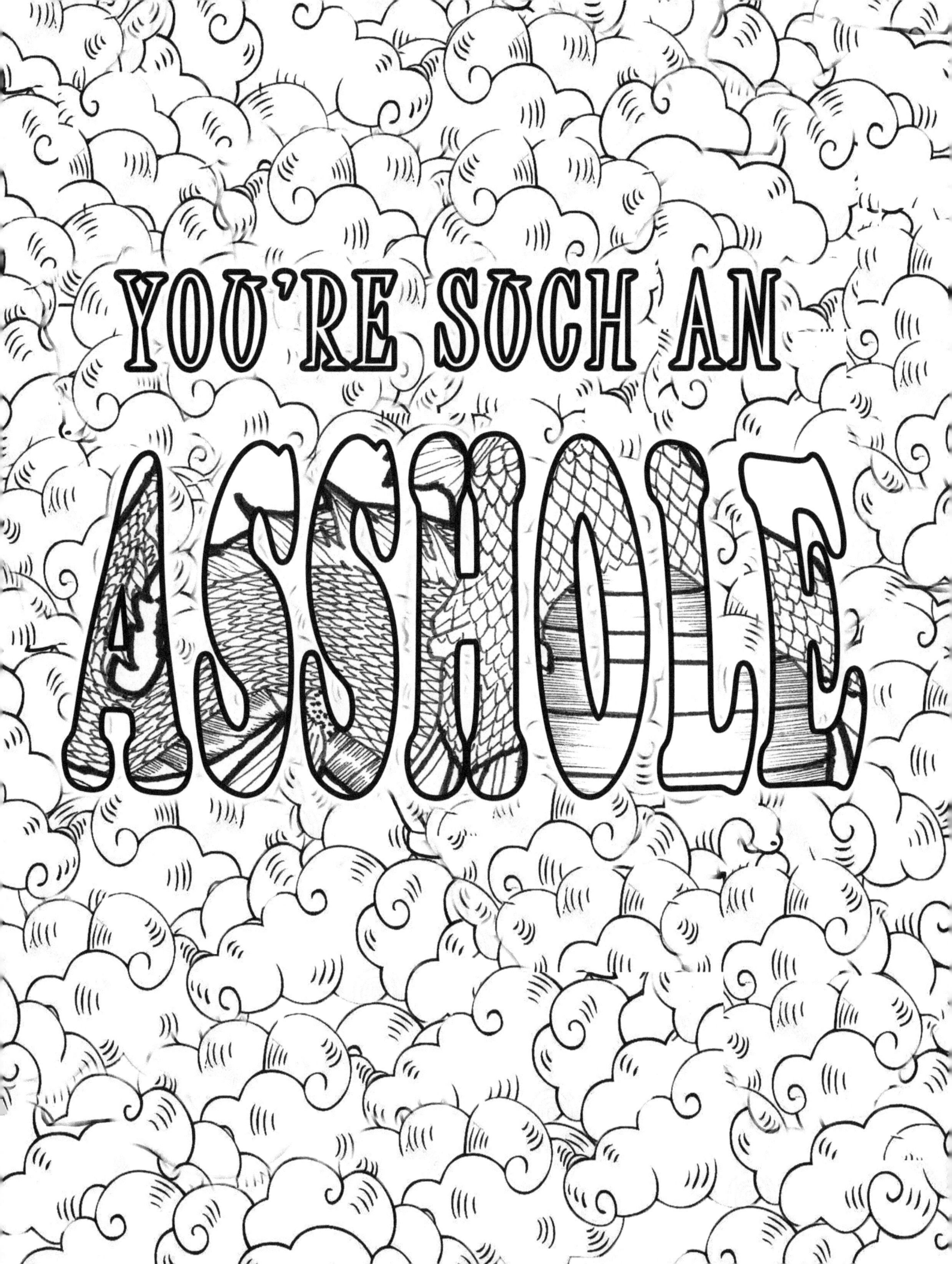

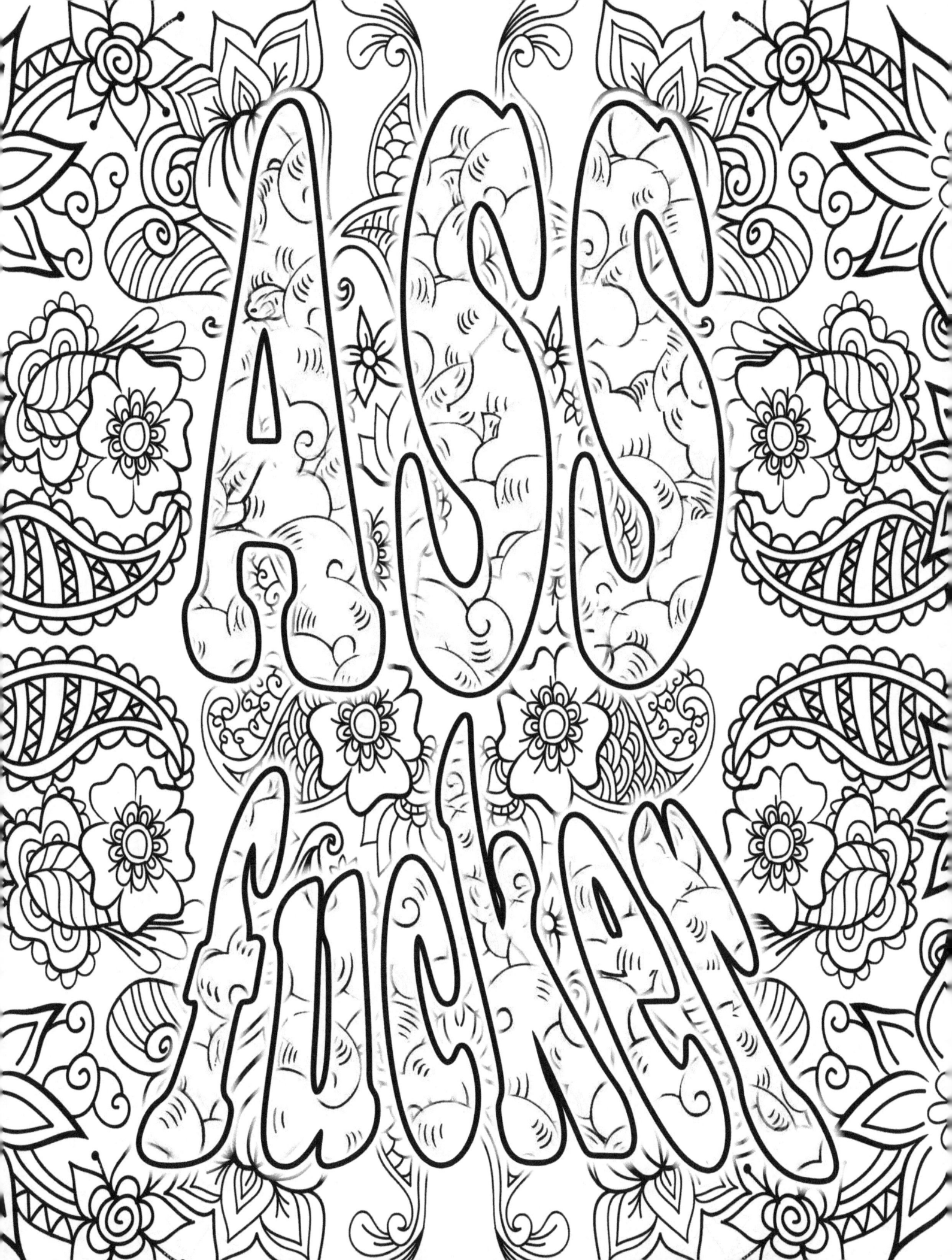

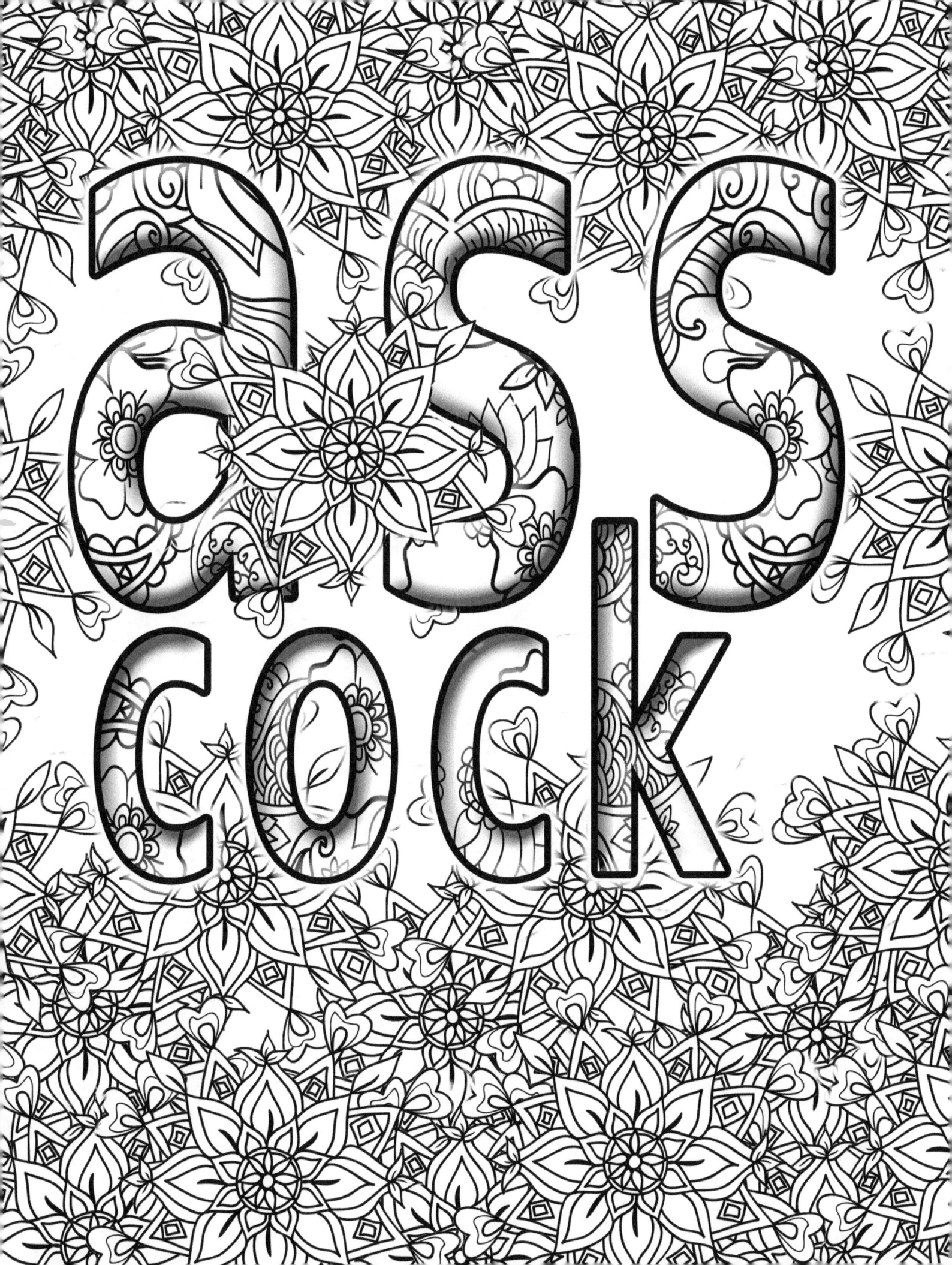

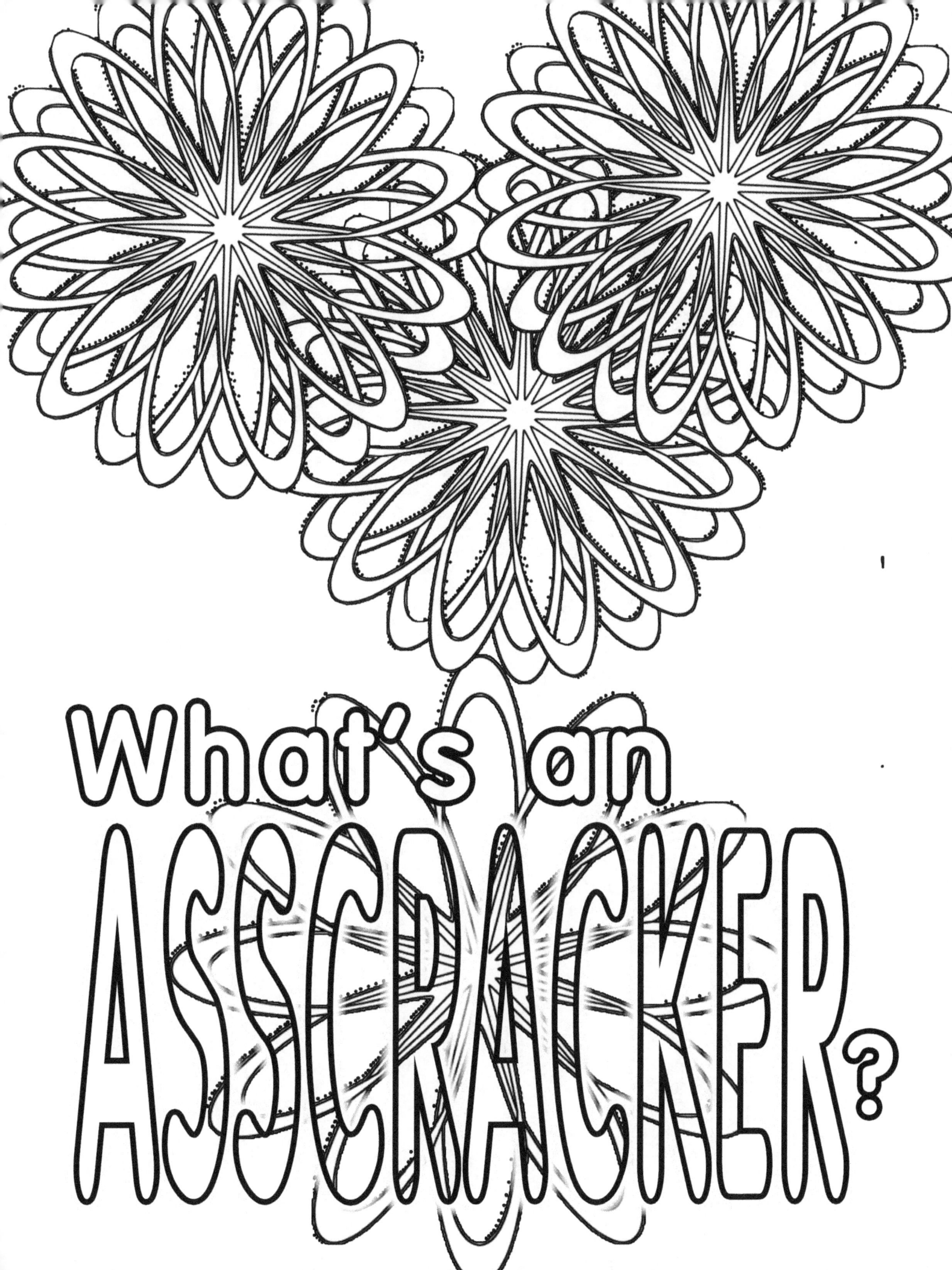

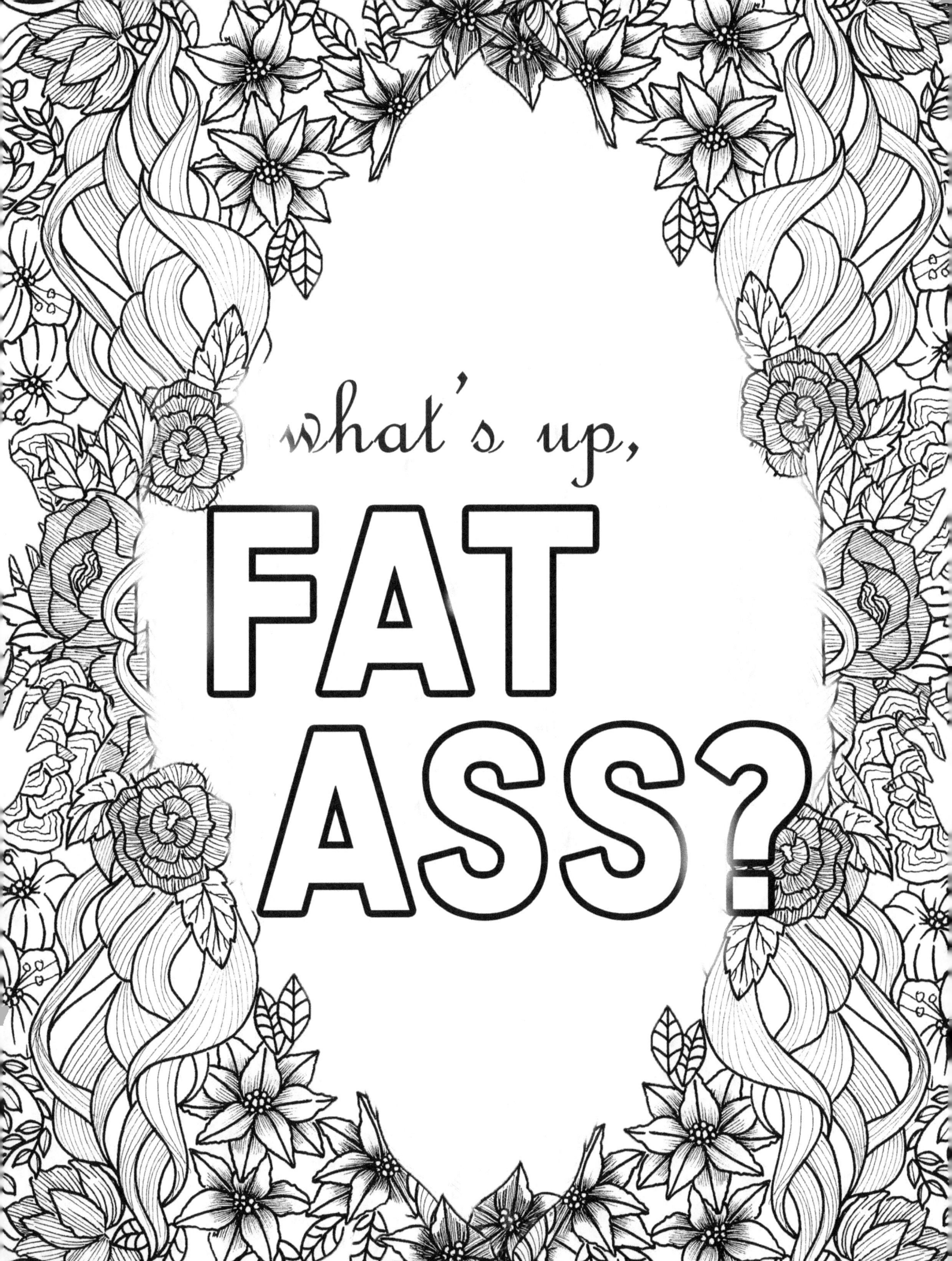

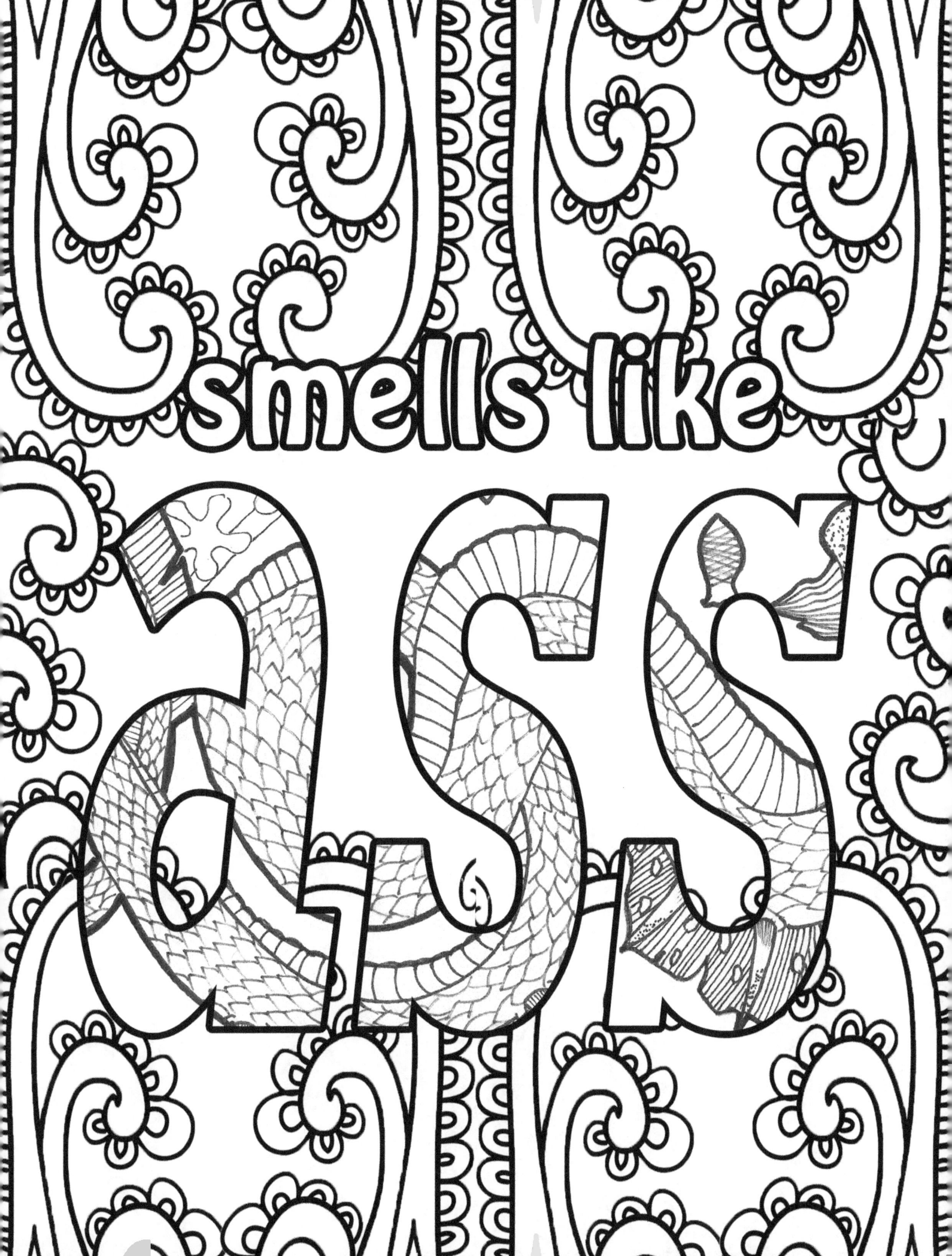

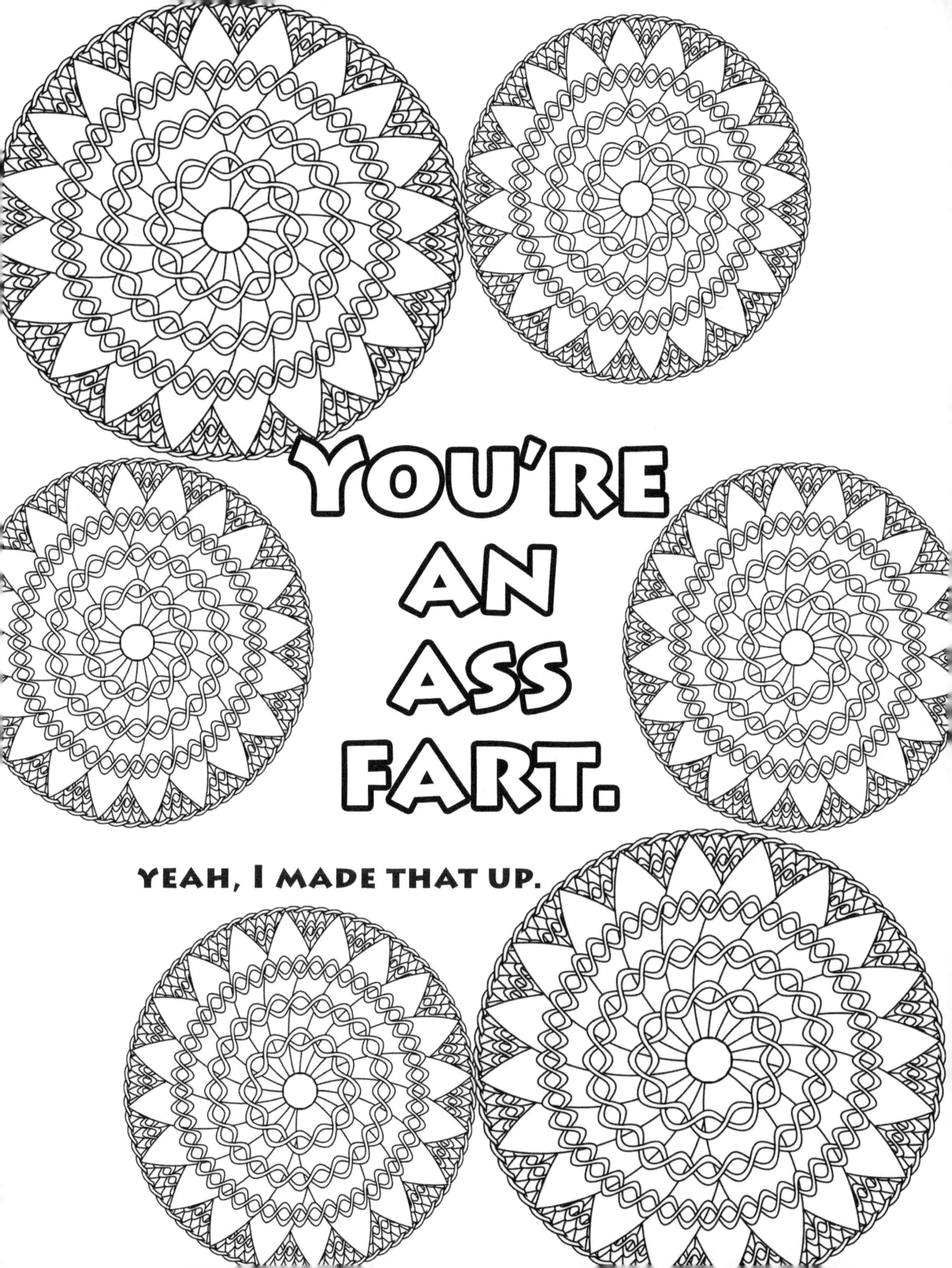

YOU'RE AN ASS FART.

YEAH, I MADE THAT UP.

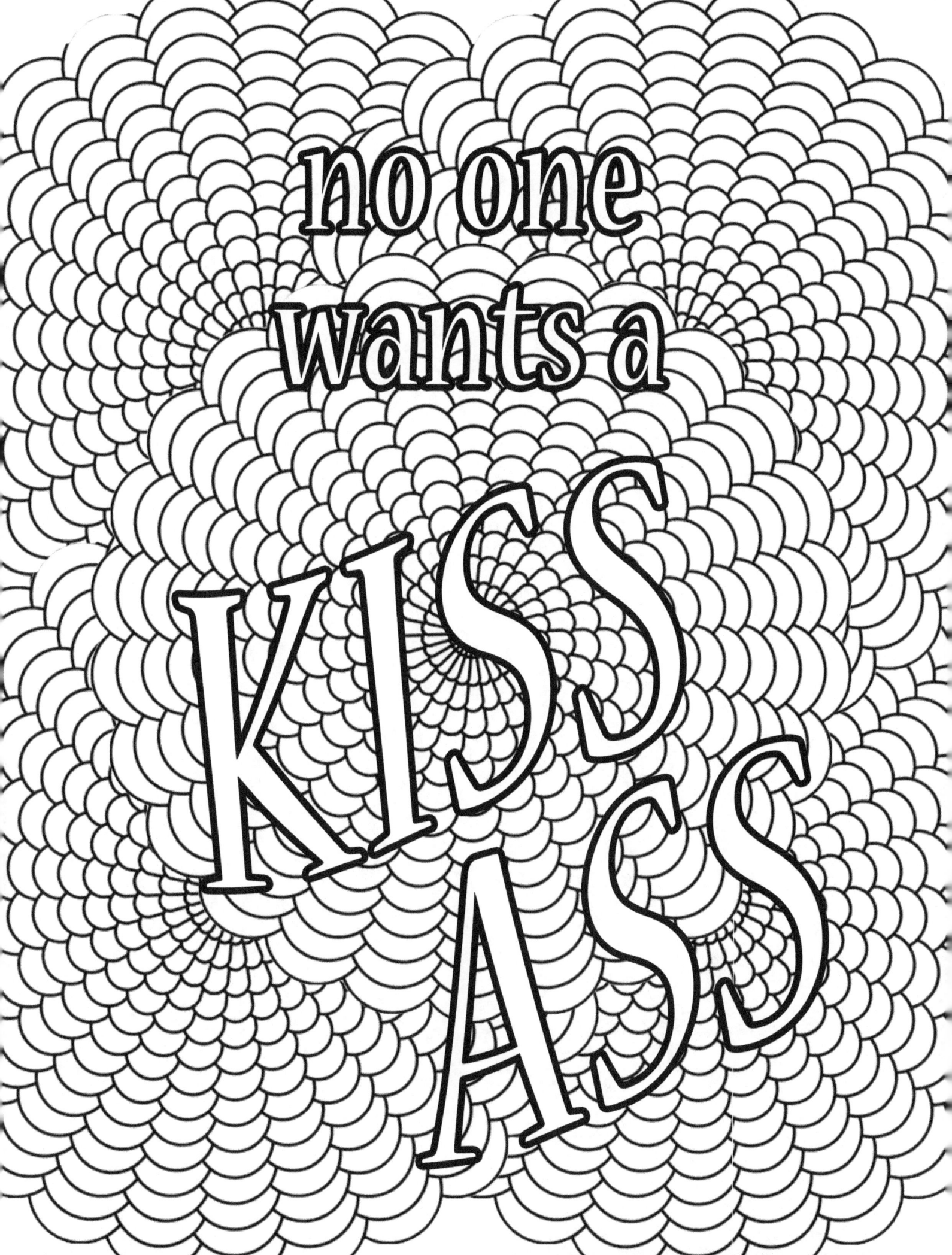

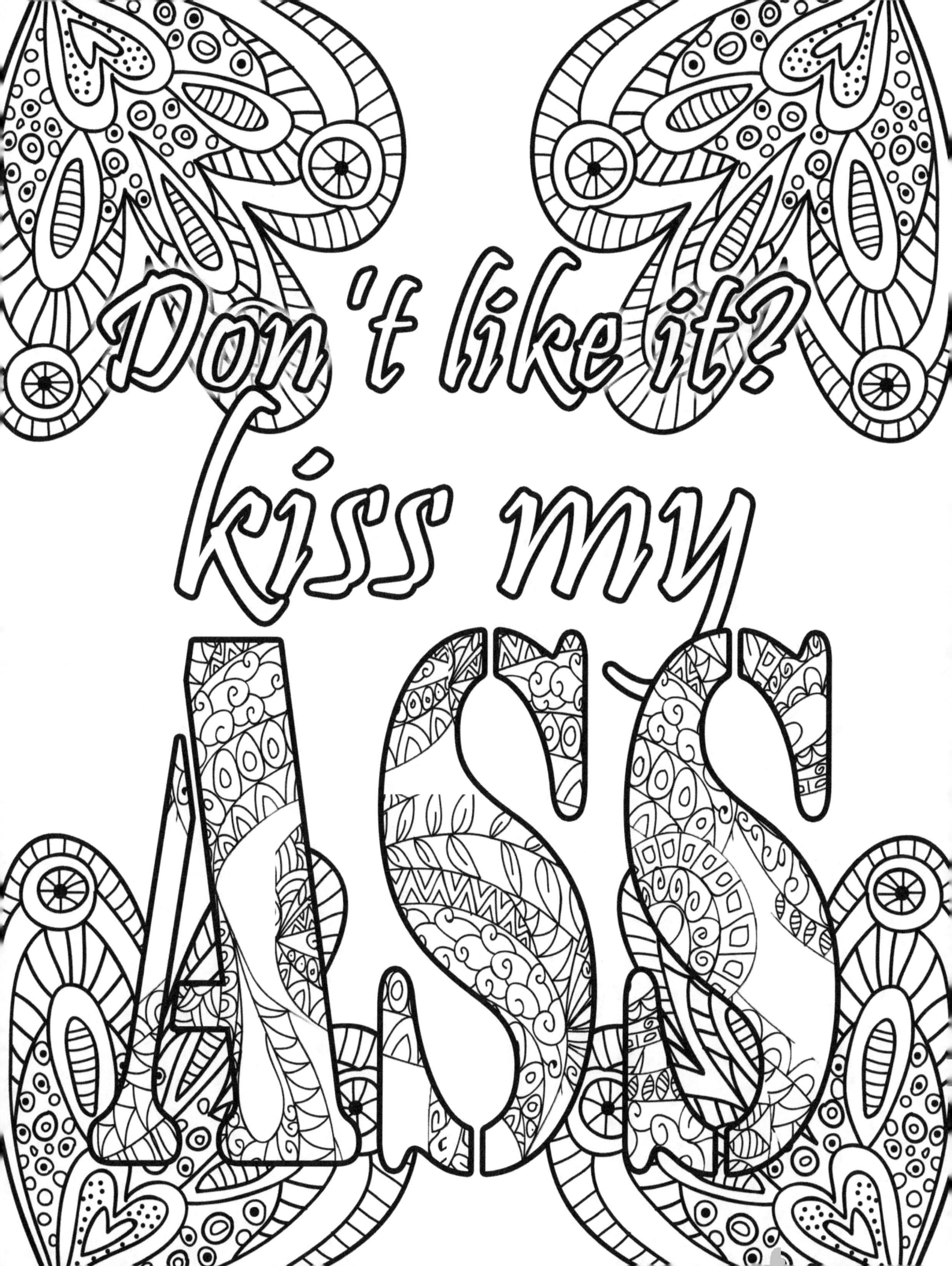

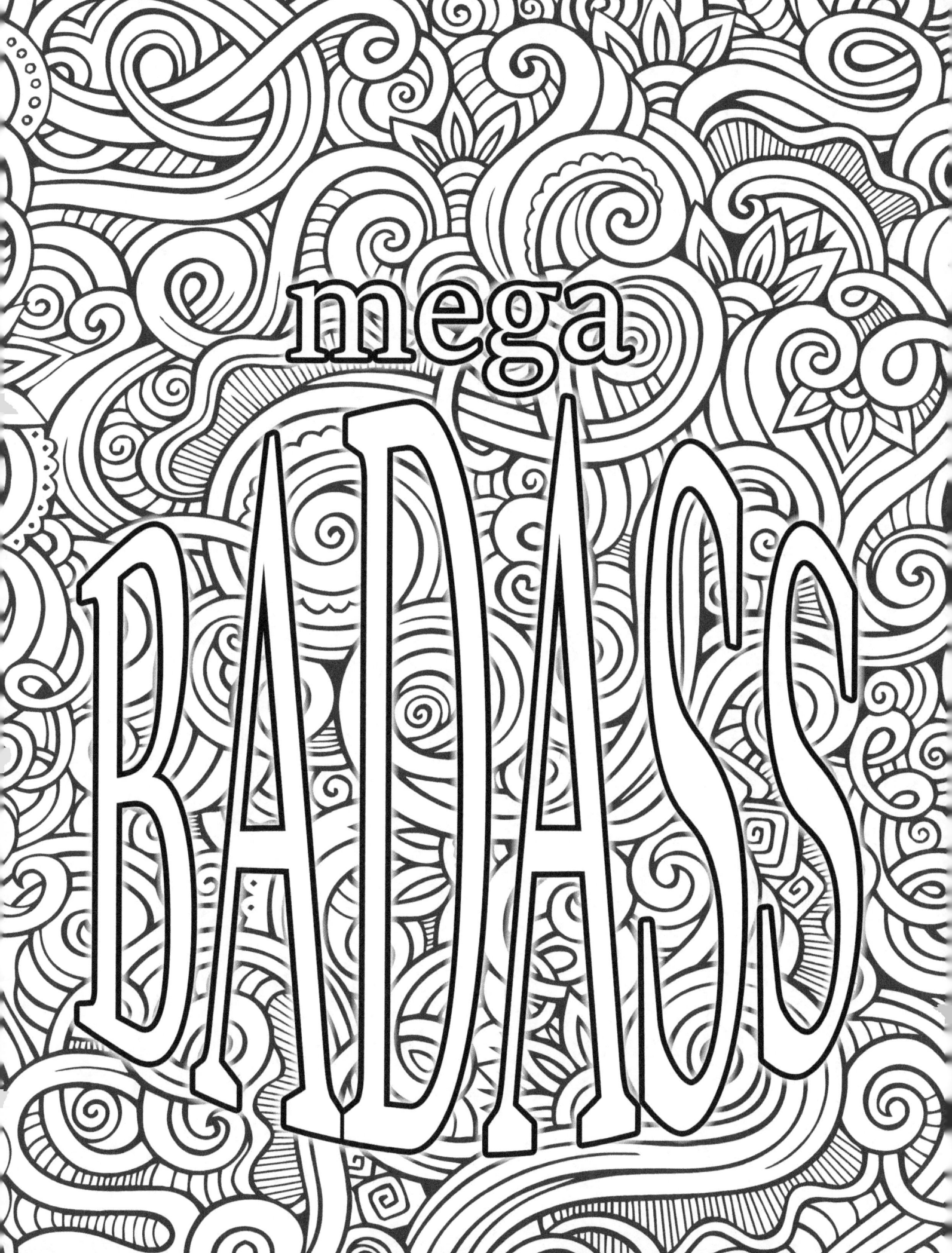

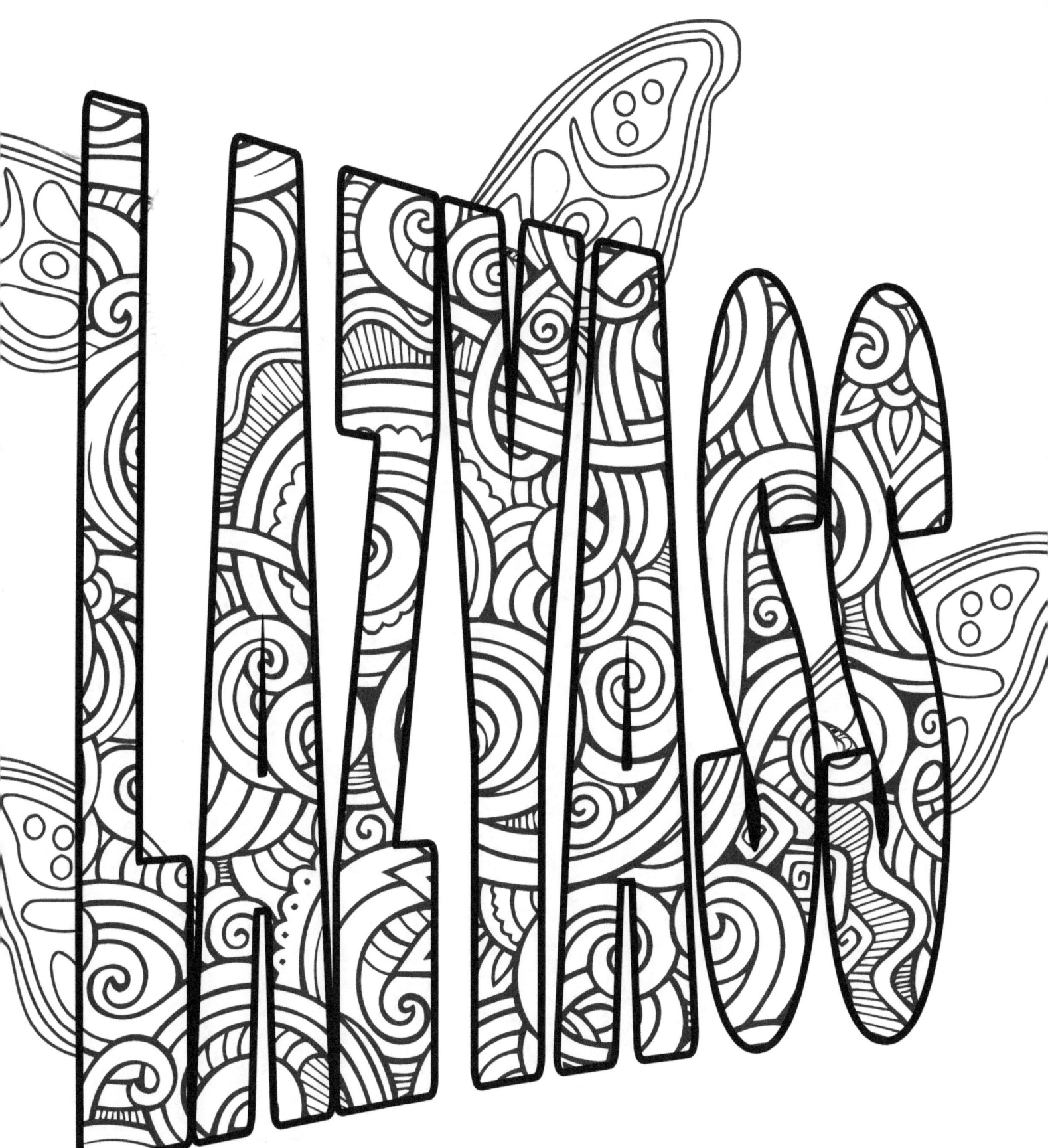

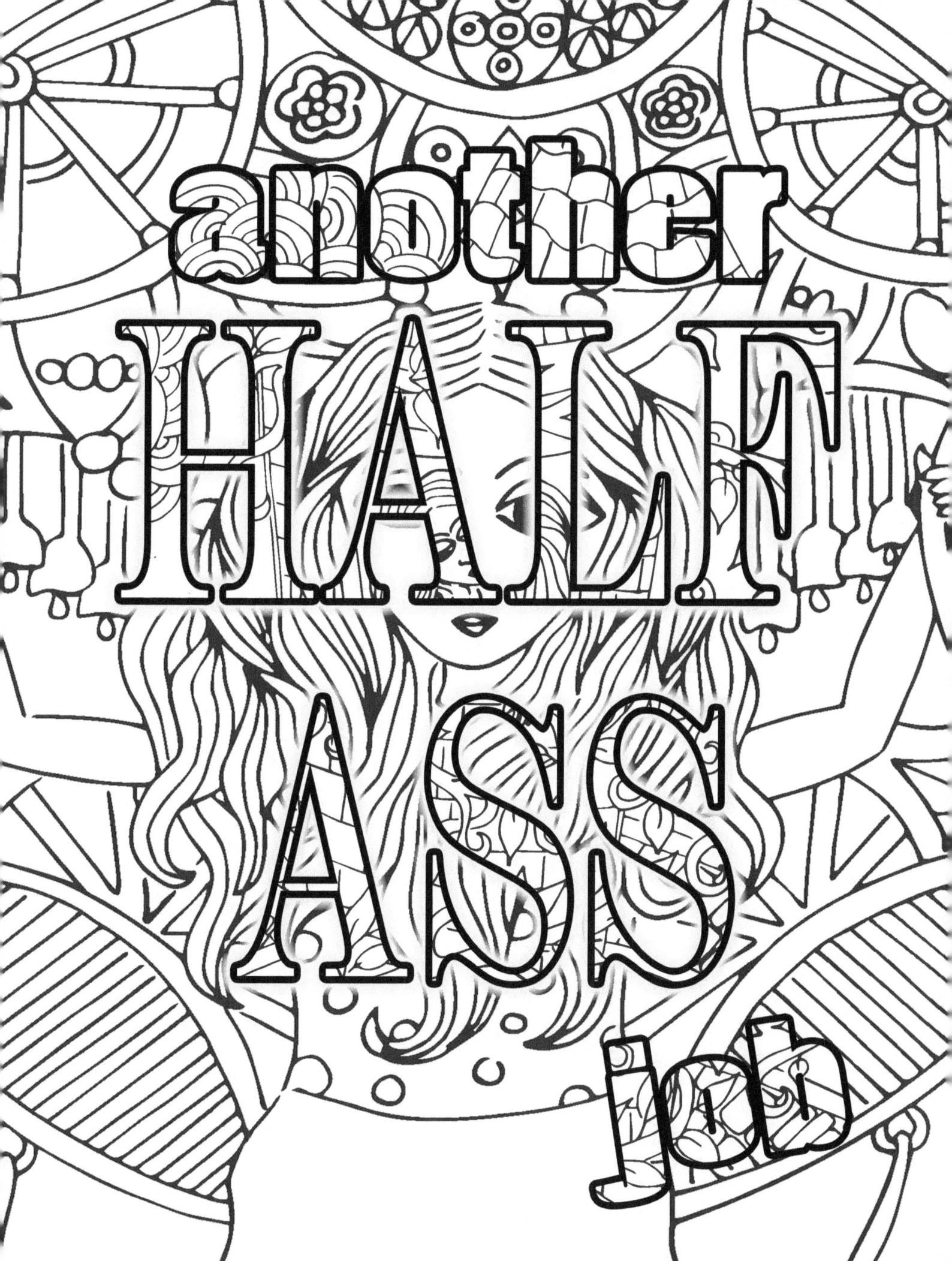

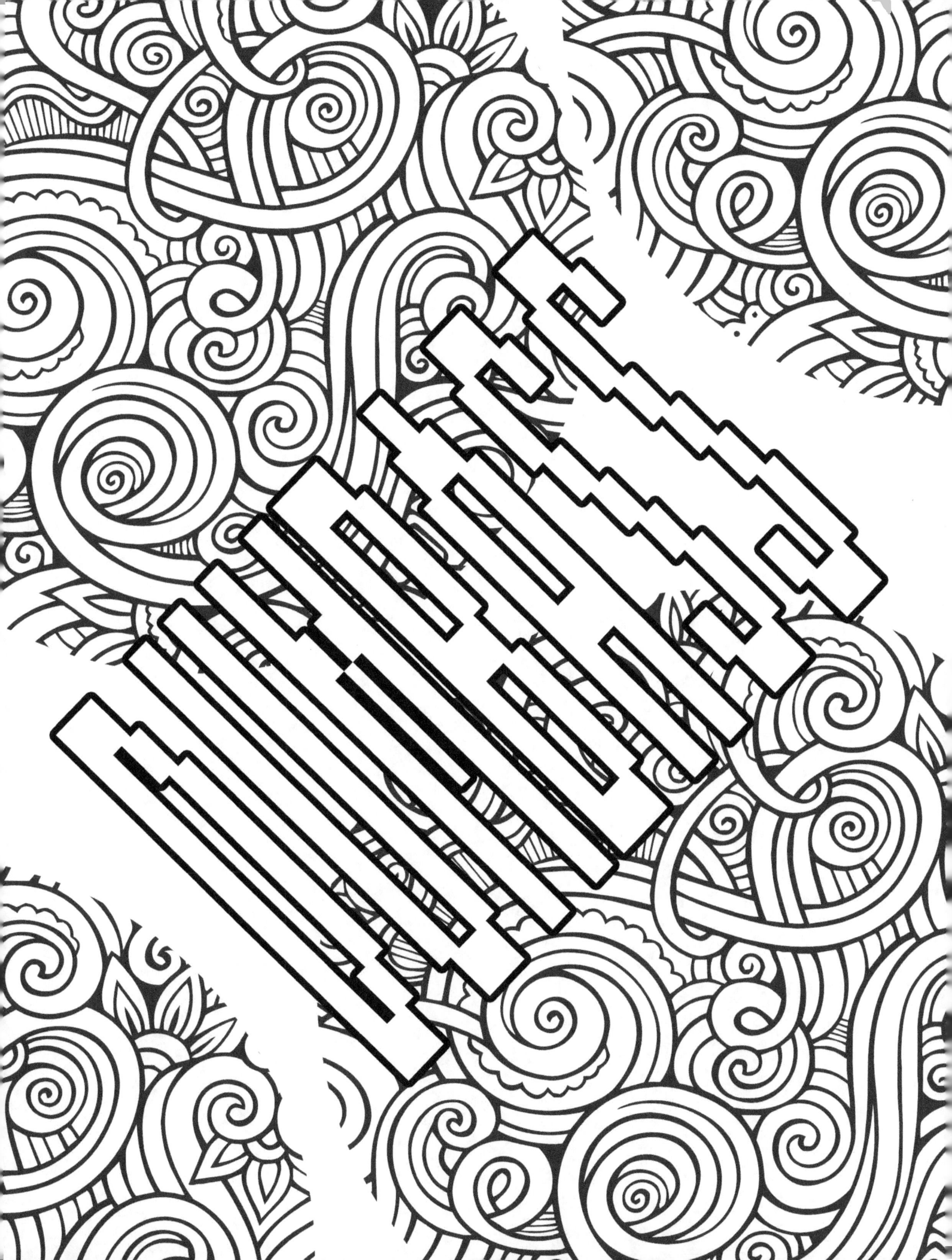

More in the Adult Coloring Book series...

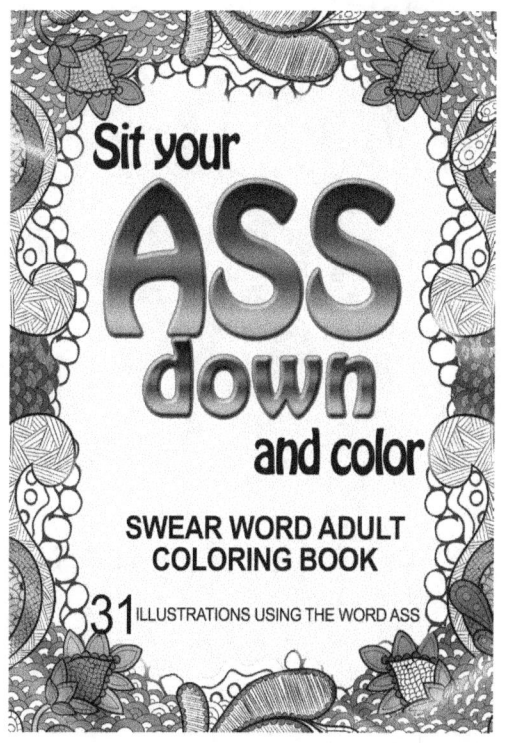

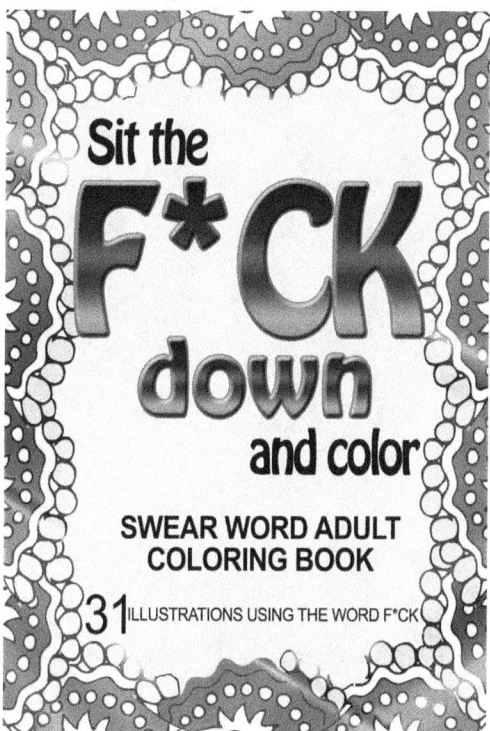

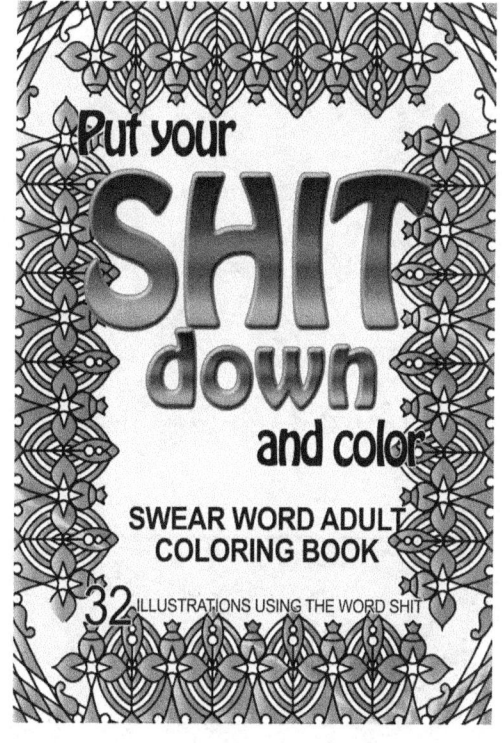

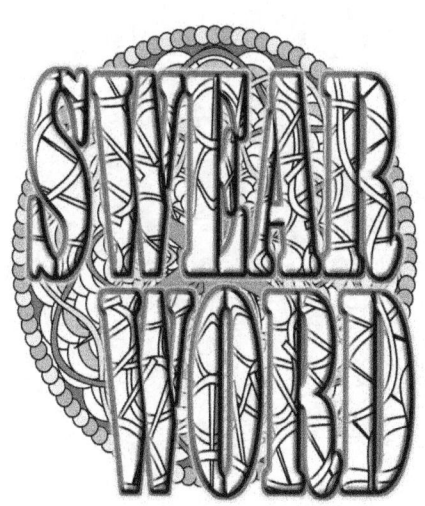

ADULT COLORING BOOK

RELAX WITH CURSE WORDS

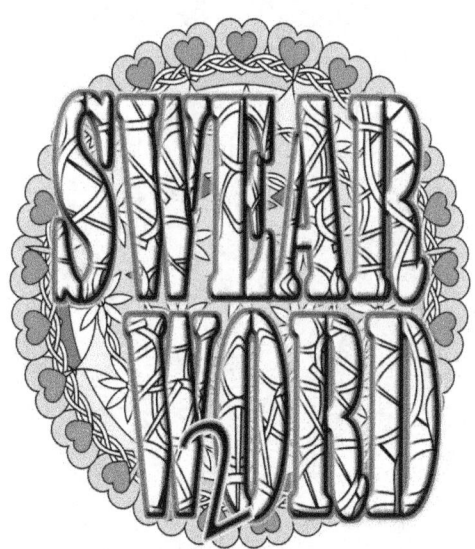

ADULT COLORING BOOK

RELAX WITH CURSE WORDS

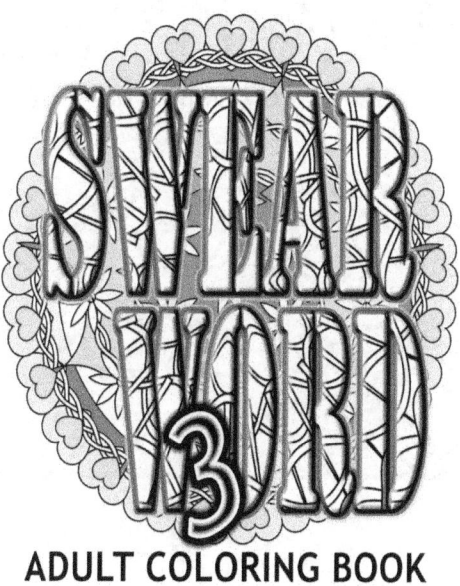

ADULT COLORING BOOK

RELAX WITH CURSE WORDS

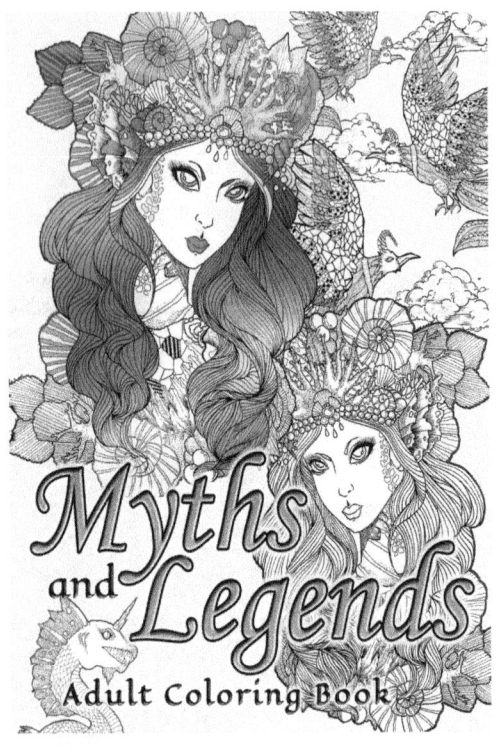

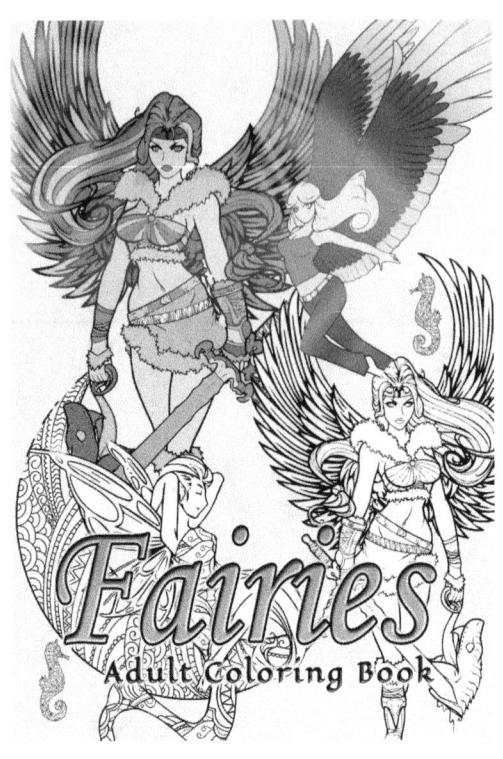

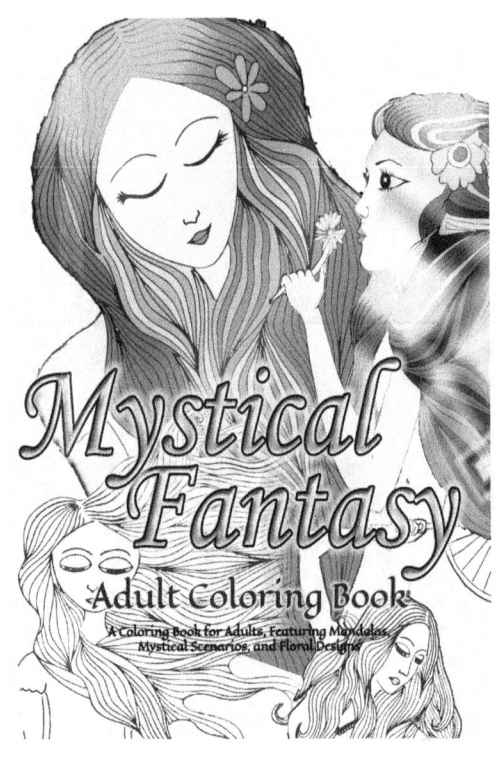

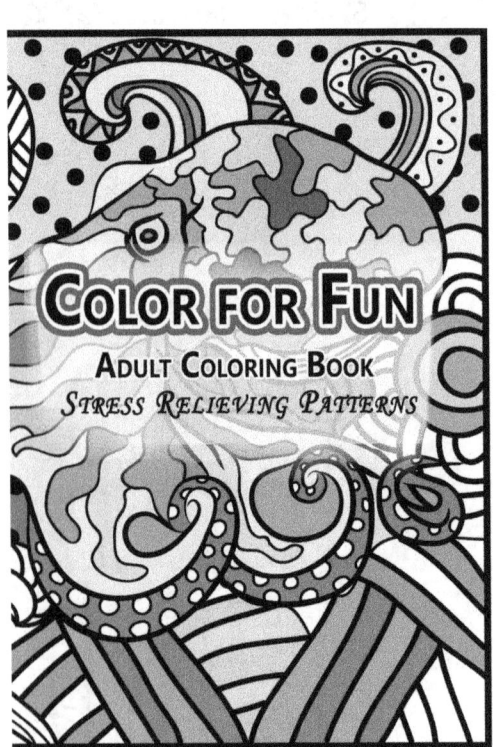

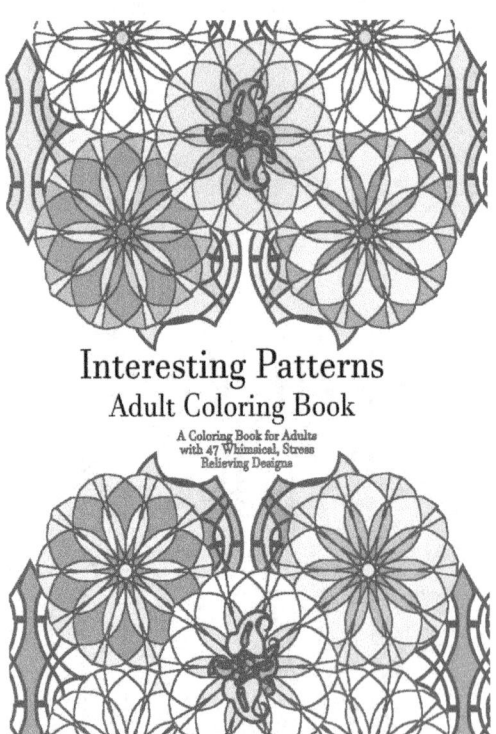

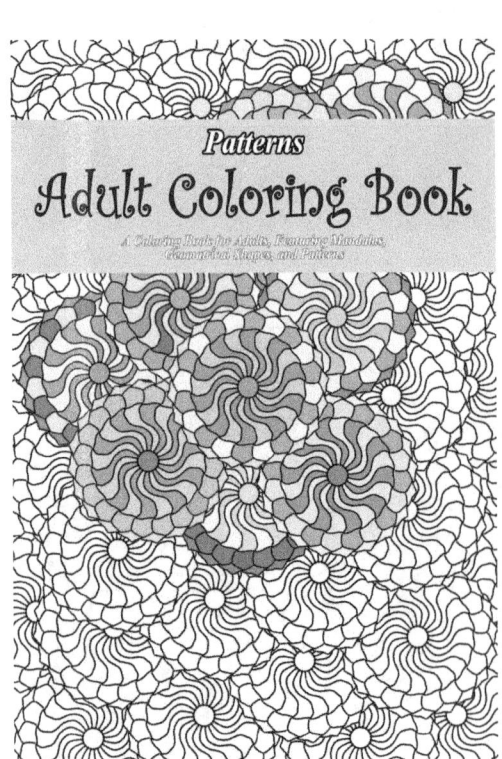

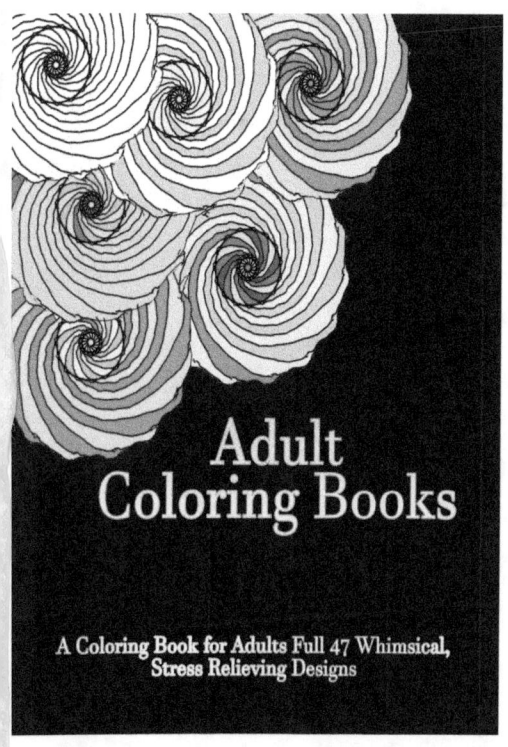

Adult Coloring Books

A Coloring Book for Adults Full 47 Whimsical, Stress Relieving Designs

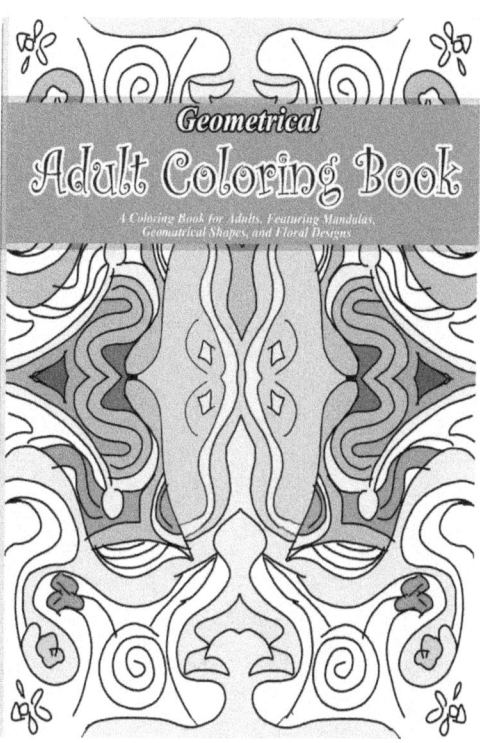

Geometrical
Adult Coloring Book

A Coloring Book for Adults, Featuring Mandalas, Geometrical Shapes, and Floral Designs

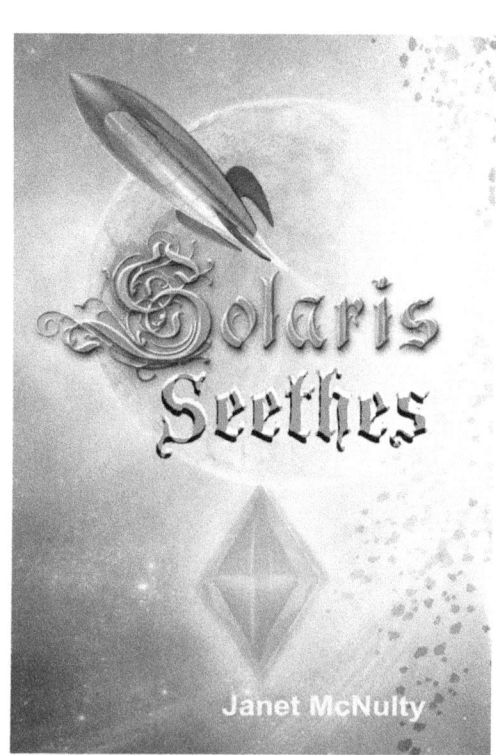

Solaris Seethes

Janet McNulty

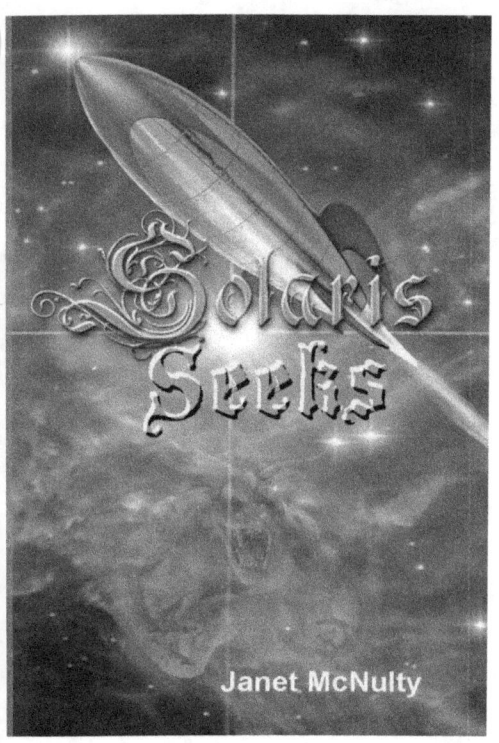

Solaris Seeks

Janet McNulty

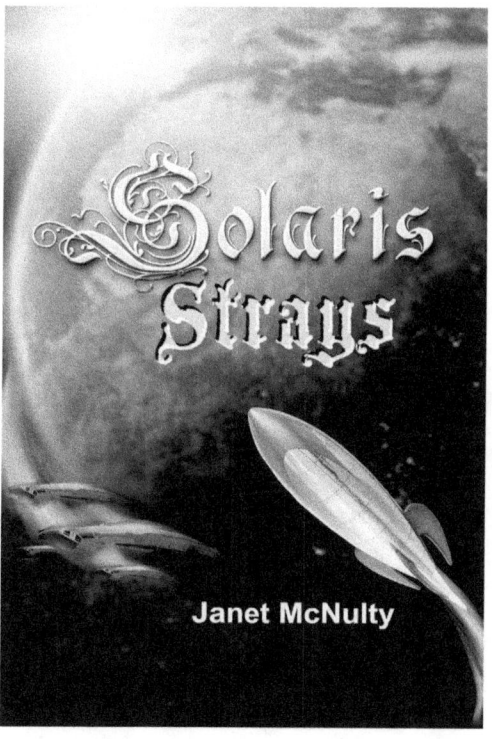

Solaris Strays

Janet McNulty

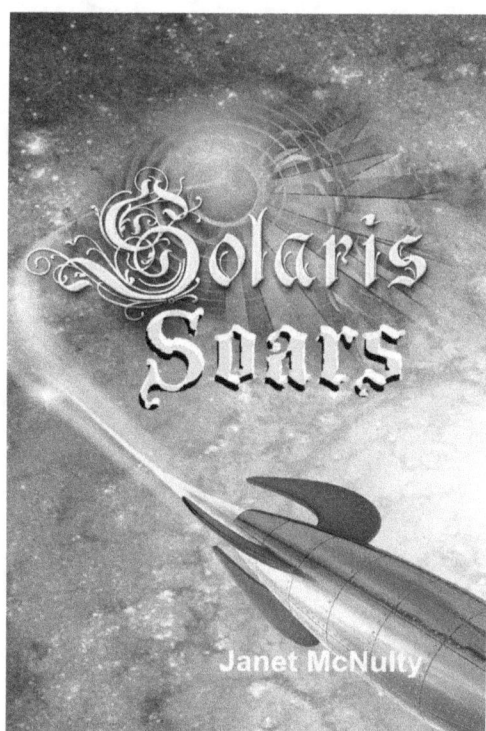

Solaris Soars

Janet McNulty

www.ingramcontent.com/pod-product-compliance
Lightning Source LLC
Chambersburg PA
CBHW080725190526

45169CB00006B/2519